DogPerfect!

- ❧ A Quick, Fun and Easy Approach

- ❧ Simple Steps You Can Apply to Everyday Life

- ❧ User-Friendly Terminology

- ❧ An Entire Encyclopedia of Canine Etiquette
  An Everyday Reference for the Rest of Us

DogPerfect

The user-friendly guide to a well-behaved dog

by Sarah Hodgson

HOWELL
BOOK
HOUSE

To Job Michael Evans,
My mentor and friend
As long as we remember, you'll never die.

Howell Book House

MACMILLAN
A Simon & Schuster Macmillan Company
1633 Broadway
New York, NY 10019

Library of Congress Cataloging-in-Publication Data

Hodgson, Sarah.
  DogPerfect / Sarah Hodgson.
    p.   cm.
  ISBN: 0-87605-534-X
  1. Dogs--Training. 2. Dogs--Behavior. I. Title
SF431.H728   1995
636.7' 0887--dc20   95–16565
                                                        CIP

Manufactured in the United States of America
10   9 8 7 6 5 4 3 2 1

Contents

Contents

Acknowledgments

There are so many people to thank! Where should I begin? First, my editor, Dominique Davis. Dependable. Understanding. Funny. Thanks for your patience, friendship and support. And to the others at Howell Book House: Top Dog Sean Frawley and his pack, Seymour Weiss, Marcy Zingler, Madelyn Larsen, Felice Primeau and Ariel Cannon. You make my visits to New York all the more fun. No matter where I am, thoughts of you make me laugh.

My clients, both dogs and people, are too many to name personally. My apologies! You have been my learning source as much as I've been your teacher. I'm lucky to have found you.

Thanks to the many people from past clients to good-hearted veterinarians, pet supply stores, groomers and other trainers who have kept my name in circulation. I would not be where I am, professionally, without you.

My friends and family. Four-legged and two. Thanks for keeping me sane.

A Welcoming Wag!

Welcome to *DogPerfect*. A simple, straightforward guidebook for you, the everyday person, and your everyday dog. Before we jump in, however, I want to clear the air about something. There is no such thing as a "Dog Perfect," no single animal that embodies it all. In fact, there are as many ideals of perfection in dogs as there are in people. Perfection, when it comes right down to it, is a very personal thing.

Are some of you reading this cross-eyed, thinking, "Perfection? If I could figure out how to get my dear puppy from peeing on the carpet or get my darling dog's snout out of the wastepaper basket, I'd be satisfied with that."

Well, whether your goals are short-term problem-solving or long-term off-lead control, with a dog or a puppy, this book outlines it all. Its lively text is fun, informative and easy to read. The everyday language can be understood by readers aged nine to ninety and can be read by the whole family. The layout simplifies my instructions and draws attention to important information unique to individual situations. As you read along, watch for:

 This indicates a note or tip I want to share with you.

This alerts you to a General Information box, where you'll learn interesting Fido facts.

When you see this sign, you'll know there's a Lesson to be learned. Quick and easy.

It's Story time. Here's where I share my and others' personal experiences to help you relate to your own situation.

You will also notice a question section after each new concept or command is described. Here I have asked questions of myself as you would of me if I were training your dog in person.

In addition to the book, you can purchase its companion video to visualize the training methods and corrective techniques. Like the book, the video is upbeat yet educational. **Ordering information is provided at the back of the book.**

One more thing. I know it might be hard for some of you to imagine, but you and your dog really do want the same things. You both want to get along with one another and be happy. While your jump-all-over-you, run-when-you-say-"come," nip-at-your-trouser Fido may appear to be having a blast, he's having no more fun than you are. He's confused. He interprets your frustrated behavior, your body language, your bark (the human yell) as interactive, not corrective. You're out of control. So instead of correcting his activities, you're encouraging them. He gets more wild. You get more frustrated. Wild. Frustrated. Wild. Frustrated. Help!!!!!

Whether this sounds too familiar or you're simply striving to preserve your dog's wonderful disposition, you'll find empathy within these pages. This book not only answers and instructs, it provides insight into the cause and effect of your relationship with your best friend.

Enjoy this book. Think of me as your coach and translator. Dogs are more fascinating when you understand them.

Why Bother Training?

Exley, named after the writer Frederick Exley, is a three-year-old German Shorthaired Pointer who lives in Brooklyn, New York. His owner rescued him from a shelter when he was a year old. Although Exley pulled on the leash, only listened to commands when the mood struck him, was destructive when his owner left for work, and was a headache around company, the relationship worked. Or so his owner thought. Until a friend pointed out that Exley wasn't so happy. His pacing and whining habits were not signs of a mentally balanced dog. Neither was the destructive chewing that went on when he was left alone. Or the pulling on the lead, which left him choking on the way to the park. That was when I entered the picture.

My first impression? Exley was a blur of excitement. Too happy. He didn't know what to do with himself. Quickly I reached for a ball and one of my Teaching Leads. Ball for Exley. Teaching Lead for my control. After just a few minutes, I discovered a highly intelligent dog who eagerly soaked up every direction I gave him. He was a dog willing to cooperate. He just didn't know what his owner wanted from him. He was like a spoiled brat crying out for some guidance. Unfortunately, it's an all-too-common problem. From Exley's point of view, he was the leader: first to greet company at the door, got attention whenever he wanted it, and led his owner to the park.

So who could solve Exley's problems? Only his owner, who had to take responsibility for creating the problem as well as for solving it. He could do all this by training. By making a commitment to give Exley direction. By becoming his leader.

And you, my readers—with your Exleys, or Fluffys, or Baileys, or Sams—I hope you can see the importance of training, too. Whether your problems are similar to the one described or not, training is still the solution. It defines the hierarchy. It puts you in charge and gives your dog the freedom to be a dog. You'll both be happier, more content with one another and less stressed out. And as this book will show, training never breaks a dog's spirit; on the contrary, it can set him free.

Chapter 1

Who Is My Dog and How Does He Learn?

This question seems pretty simple. Who is your dog? Take a look. Big or small? Pup or grown-up? A special breed from a specific country? How about your dog's ancestors—did they do anything fancy for their keep, like hunting, herding, or pulling a sled?

Who is your dog? *Arlene Oraby.*

Your answers to these questions will shape how you map your way through this book. Dogs are as individual as snowflakes. In addition, you are another element in your dog's behavior and training. Each of you has different lifestyles, schedules and social commitments. To help you, I'll need to cover all angles. You and your dog are a unique pair.

DOG PSYCHOLOGY

I can feel some of you rolling your eyes saying "Great, I've got this nutty dog running my life who, in addition, is unique to me. Very poetic. But how can that help me train him?" Well, nutty or not, the first step in teaching your dog how to behave is understanding him. He's not human. He doesn't think, look or feel like you. He isn't born knowing a house from a hole in the ground, a rug from the grass, or a stick from a table leg. He's a dog.

The most important thing to keep in mind as you bring your older dog up to snuff or raise that pup is that he thinks of you (and your family) as a dog. Yes, dogs are the quintessential product of our domestication efforts. We did such a good job that they think of us as being just like them. Quite a compliment. Therefore, the first step in this training process will be to make yourself think and act like a dog. It's fun, I promise. Let's start. ❧ *Tip: Humans and dogs have some clear-cut differences that will influence how you relate to each other. Three, to be exact. (There are some similarities, too, but I'll address those later.)*

The Leadership Principle

Dogs are not terribly democratic. Instead, they live in a hierarchy, in which group members are classed according to their leadership potential.

Number One ("The Leader") acts beyond questioning and is respected by all. ❧ *Tip: That should be you. Is it?*

Number Two answers to no one but One.

Number Three directs all but One and Two. And so on . . . .

To be truly influential in your dog's behavior, guess where you must align yourself? If a family is involved, your dog must learn that two-legged dogs rule four-legged ones. No ifs, ands or buts!

In a family, two-legged dogs rank above four-legged dogs.

The Attention Factor

Dogs love attention! They're motivated by it. And they don't care whether it's negative or positive. If an action gets a reaction, they'll repeat it.

Imagine this homecoming . . . . You enter the house, and your dog goes wild. You want to run for cover, but she would follow you. Whether you push her off or hug her, what are you communicating? That's right . . . attention!

🐾 *Note: Pay attention to the behavior you want to encourage—for example, when your dog is chewing on a bone, lying down, or sitting quietly at your side.*

Doglish

We speak English, dogs speak Doglish. Since we are striving to understand them, we must become fluent in their native tongue. Words don't count anymore. Now it's eye contact, body language and tone. Here's a quick lesson.

Eye Contact
Can your dog get you to look at him on cue (with a bark, paw scratch, head rub, whine, or stare) more often than you can get him to look to you? (Are

you left calling "FIDO, COME!!!" as your dog races away?) If so, you're being trained by your dog. It's embarrassing, I know, but you're not alone. One of our first goals will be to shift this equation and get those dreamy dog eyes focused on you!

Body Language

Do you bend over a lot when correcting or commanding your dog? Does she ignore you or cringe and run for cover? When you bend over, she interprets your posture as playful (she'll get more excited), submissive (she'll ignore you), or extremely threatening (she'll freak). You don't want her to have any of the preceding reactions; they're too intense. When communicating, assume what I call the Peacock Position: Stand tall, throw your shoulders back, and communicate with authority.

Stand tall, relax, and throw your shoulders back like a proud peacock! *Sally Sarsfield.*

Here are some rules about body language:

RELAX   A tense posture communicates confusion or excitement. Let's say you meet someone on the street and your dog braces for the bounce. Your tension would communicate a mutual anticipation. Instead, remind yourself to relax so that you're able to prepare a quick correction.

GET AHEAD   If your dog is in front of you, guess who's not in charge? You. To communicate direction or disapproval, you must position yourself in front of your dog. The leader always leads.

STAY CENTERED   Suppose that your dog barks wildly at the door and you, disturbed from a quiet nap on the couch, jump up and start yelling. Since a yell counts for a bark in dogland, your dog will naturally feel reinforced for her alerting instincts. Bark-yell-bark-yell!!!! When your dog gets nervous, stay centered and calm. Soon you'll learn how to correct your dog with authority, not reinforcement!

DETACH   Some people take their dog's behavior too personally. When a dog behaves poorly in a social situation, the owner can become giddy listing every excuse for the dog's reaction. This only worsens the problem, because rambling and bent body postures communicate chaos and confusion. When your dog acts up, calm down. Detach yourself from the situation. Keep your cool, and take a deep breath. Your dog needs a level-headed leader—and it's up to you to be one!

TONE   I'll share a little secret with you. Tone is 75 percent of dog training. The lower you can make your voice naturally, the more respect you'll get. Dogs sense four tones: happy tones, directional tones, corrective tones, and high-pitched squeals.

Use *happy tones* to praise good behavior. Some dogs need more enthusiasm than others do. Test your dog to see what level works.

The *directional tone* is your commanding voice. Make sure you're not offering an option (Are you saying "SIT" so that it sounds like a question? Listen to how you ask your dog to obey you.) Are you repeating yourself—saying, "SIT-SIT-SIT"? Both sound different to your dog than a clear, flat "SIT!") 🐾 *Tip: Hey Parents! Whether your kids are two or twelve, you'll need to help them out teaching the dog. Make a habit of over-enunciating your commands. Your kids will follow your lead, and the dog will respond better to the whole family.*

Let's look at *corrective tones*. Are you a yeller? Well, guess what? Yellers makes matters worse. Sure, some dogs cringe and crawl away on their belly, but that's not a sign of understanding, it's a sign of terror. And who'd want to terrorize their helpless doggy? Not you. So what's a good alternative? How can you communicate disapproval? First, use the Peacock Rule: Stand tall. Next, act really ashamed of your dog: "WHAT DID YOU DO? SHAME ON YOU!" Acting indignant will get you further than going berserk.

❧ *Tip: Caught Red-Handed: If you catch your dog in a negative thought process, like sniffing the counter or approaching a tissue basket, say "NO!" in a very cross tone as you stamp your foot. Interrupting the thought process often eliminates the action.*

A *high-pitched squeal* is the only sound that can work against you. It communicates fear, confusion or submission. Kids often squeal, as do many women. If you can help yourself stop, do. Otherwise you'll just have to over-emphasize on every other training suggestion to make up for the loss.

THE SAME, ONLY DIFFERENT

Now that we've listed the differences, let's talk similarities. Yes, this is for real; after all, we're animals, too. There are actually lots of parallels. Let's start with three: *personality profiles*, *breed differences*, and *the age issue*.

Personality Profiles

Some people may think that only humans have a real personality. Anyone who has ever had a dog knows better. Dogs, like us, have their own personalities. Some are extremely funny. I call this rowdy bunch *The Comedians.* They can be frustrating as heck, constantly dancing on the edge of good behavior, but in your most serious or sad moments, they'll make you laugh. Then we have *The Eager Beavers,* the dogs many of us dream of. They'll do anything that warrants approval. Sounds fantastic, but they'll be bad, too, if that gets attention, so even the Eager Beavers can find themselves on the "B" list if their owners aren't careful. There are also *The Sweet Peas* of the planet. Quiet souls who prefer the sidelines over the spotlight. Taking the sweet thing a step too far are those dogs who are *Truly Timid*. Almost anything will freak them out. Poor creatures, they require a lot of understanding. And then there is *The Boss*. This fellow thinks a little too highly of himself. He needs lots of training to tame his egotism. Take a look at where your dog fits in, because like us, they all learn differently!

Understanding your dog's character
will broaden your appreciation of it.

Breed Differences

Breeds are the equivalent of cultures. Same species, different styles. The American Kennel Club recognized 141 different breeds when I wrote this book; the number is growing. Besides looking different, each has individual instincts and drives that make it unique—instincts and drives we helped create. The Doberman Pinscher was bred by the Germans for protection; the Alaskan Malamute, by the Eskimos to help them pull their sleds; the Shih Tzu, for companionship.

So what about your warm bundle? What were her ancestors doing? With few exceptions, a dog's skills are no longer necessary to our survival, but don't tell that to your dog. Her instincts and breeding still make her think her skills are very much in demand. Finding out what they were will help you understand how she's viewing her role in the world today.

"So what if every dog is different—can't they all adapt?"

Yes, with training. But adaptation is relative. Certain breeds can adapt only so much. For example, suppose you're having a house party. A Golden Retriever in that situation would consider the opportunity marvelous for making new friends and showing off her latest tennis ball collection. Maybe a bit too cheery, but she'll mesh just fine. A German Shepherd, however, bent on keeping track of her territory, might suffer career stress watching the comings and goings. With training, she may become more accepting, but don't expect her to lie belly-up at just anyone's feet. Only yours will do. Training helps you get a handle on your dog's instincts, but you can never eliminate them completely.

THE GROUPS

In the United States, breeds are categorized into seven groups: Sporting, Hound, Working, Terrier, Non-Sporting, Toy and Herding. These groups are organized by the American Kennel Club according to shared characteristics. After determining which group your dog is a member of, read the following corresponding description to determine some predictable character traits. 🐾 *Tip: Breeders, trainers and veterinarians can help determine what breed your dog is if you're not sure.*

If you have a mixed-breed dog, don't worry! Your job is a little more adventurous. Try to identify the mix; then read over each group description. Then study your dog's behavior, and decide where it fits in.

The Sporting Group

Originally bred to spend entire days in the fields seeking out and collecting land- and waterfowl for their masters, this bunch is an energetic, loyal, happy lot who thrive on group interaction. Trusting, friendly and bright, they take to training well and generally view all strangers as potential friends. These easy-going dogs make excellent family pets, but prolonged isolation does upset them. Isolated, they'll develop diversionary habits like destructive chewing, barking, digging or jumping. They are annoyingly enthusiastic when left untrained. Examples are Labrador and Golden Retrievers, Irish Setters, German Shorthaired Pointers and Cocker Spaniels.

The Hound Group

These guys were bred to pursue game, using their eyes (sighthounds) or their noses (scenthounds). They are dogs with a mission! Active, lively and rugged, they make fun-loving, gentle pets—with an independent streak. Not bred to look to man for direction, they usually don't. Consequently, training them can be slow and challenging; they'd rather trail a rabbit than do sit-stays. Generally sweet, lively and tolerant, hounds thrive on family involvement, and accept children and strangers with ease. Examples are Basset Hounds, Greyhounds, Beagles and Rhodesian Ridgebacks.

The Working Group

This is the most diversified group in terms of their breed functions (some pull sleds, others guard flocks, and others protect the homestead). They do, however, have one common bond: They were all bred to serve man, helping him survive and advance along the evolutionary scale. As pets, the working breeds are still very serious about their roles as workers and need a serious commitment to training. Intelligent, fearless and dignified, they can make devoted, loyal pets. Misunderstood, isolated or untrained, they'll be unhappy, nervous and, in some cases, overly aggressive. Examples are Rottweilers, Mastiffs, Doberman Pinschers and Siberian Huskys.

The Herding Group

These dogs were bred to move flocks and herds. Agile and alert, they're always on the lookout and will settle for kids or bikes if sheep aren't available. Easy to train, they are devoted to their families and not prone to roaming. They can be protective, preferring family members to outsiders. Isolated or ignored, they may become timid, bark, or develop pacing habits. Examples are German Shepherds, Collies, Pulik and Corgis.

The Terrier Group

Originally bred to control the varmint population, these dogs are a self-assured, spirited and lively bunch. Agile and independent, they're always ready to face a diversion and, outdoors, need to be leashed. They make great pets for all but the control freaks and often leave their owners marveling at their spunk and good humor. When untrained or overisolated, however, these little acrobats can become chronic barkers, destructive chewers, urine makers or territorial aggressors over objects, food and other animals. Examples are Bull Terriers, West Highland White Terriers, Miniature Schnauzers and Scottish Terriers.

The Non-Sporting Group

Unlike other groups, this bunch has little consistency of personality because these dogs were all bred for different tasks. Some take to training better than others do. Many were originally bred for specific work, but when that work was no longer necessary, they became companions. If you've got a dog from this category, you can determine more about him from breed-specific books. Examples are Bulldogs, Dalmatians, Bichon Frises and Standard and Miniature Poodles.

The Toy Group

These little guys were bred for one thing and one thing only: to be companions! In keeping with their ancestry, they continue to perfect the art of being adorable. Because they are playful and affectionate, it's easy to neglect training toys, but owner beware! Without direction, they can become quite tyrannical, ruling the house with constant barking and snapping. To get the most from these critters, train them! Examples are Chihuahuas, Yorkshire Terriers, Pomeranians and Maltese.

The Age Issue

Age is a big thing. If there's a pup nibbling on your shoelace, bless you. By starting to train the puppy when she is young, you can condition a lot of good habits before the bad ones set in. Pups are a lot like us: As babies they're sensitive to the impressions of their environment and act according to the acknowledgment and consistency they receive from you.

Here's an example of how easy it is to confuse a pup. Pie, a five-month-old Welsh Corgi–Jack Russell Terrier mix lives happily with his two adult

SMALL-DOG SYNDROME

Anyone who has ever shared their life with a small dog will tell you they're adorable, especially when they're puppies. Spoiling them comes naturally. After all, their behavior is so miniaturized it's rarely a problem. Living the unstructured life, however, and being doted on night and day, is just as harmful for them. Intelligent little creatures, they conclude they must be Top Dog since there are no rules to follow and everyone is bowing to their every desire. The result is what I call Small-Dog Syndrome. Here are three typical personality developments:

- The Chronic Yapper: This one's in charge of all household activities!
- The Nipper: This one can't be disturbed when eating, chewing or resting!
- The Growler: Basically, these dogs are brats who'd be happy to fight you to have their way!

So treat your little guys like dogs, not play toys. And remember: when well-trained, they can be selectively spoiled!

owners. Well-intending and conscientious, they read every book. They handle most situations with calm and ease, but Pie still has one major problem: He was born with springs in his legs. Though they've tried to resolve his jumping problem, Pie keeps it up. Why? First the cute factor comes into play. Every time he jumps for attention, guess what? He gets it. Next, though the wife ignores jump-man Pie when she comes in, the husband, well, he can't resist. Pie gets a mixed message. Whenever somebody new enters, he must determine whether they'll be more like Mom or more like Dad. Pie also jumps for scraps, and sometimes he gets lucky. The optimum reinforcer. Now can you see why Pie spends more time on two legs than on four? (If you're experiencing this problem, stay tuned. A step-by-step solution is provided in Chapter 6.)

Pie. *Cathy Heiber.*

For those of you with older pups or dogs, don't be discouraged. It's never too late. Your job, however, is a little more of a challenge. Here's the equation: The older the dog, the stronger the habits. When the habit is sitting for attention or coming when called, everyone's happy. But when the habit is shredding the morning newspaper or trouncing the children, that's not so delightful.

So where does that leave you? Let me end this chapter with a thought: Your dog is not responsible for her habits; you are! As a pup, she simply did what got recognition. Some of the best owners have the worst dogs. Why? Because they start off with a bright, curious puppy who's naturally into everything, but instead of training her, they run about cleaning up after each escapade. How does a pup interpret this? As attention, of course. And what did I say about attention? Any action that gets a reaction will be repeated. So as a grown-up dog, what'll she be doing? Exactly what once got her such glorious recognition. Except it's not so funny after a while. The behavior gets stale and frustrating. Now the owners must do a little back pedaling to bring her up to snuff.

Whatever your dog's age, you're doing both of you a favor by consulting this book. In addition to training, you'll need to consult Chapter 6 and work through some of the problem-solving techniques. But before you begin, do just one thing: Forgive your dog her meager transgressions. She is only doing what you taught her.

KIDS AND PUPS

Aside from some obvious differences, young puppies and children are a lot alike. They both need supervision because as youngsters they have tons of energy and a budding curiosity in the world around them. In addition, they have a natural tendency to test their superiors. Remember this as your blood pressure is rising. Nothing they do is out of spite. Correcting a young pup from mouthing, nipping and exploring makes about as much sense as yelling at a one-year-old for grabbing your hair. They can't understand what they're doing yet, so what's the point of losing your temper? It only makes them more afraid and anxious, and anxious puppies are even more oral and nervous! So relax. Tolerence, patience and loving understanding are key in raising your puppy. Just like kids, they'll be grown up before you know it! For more on this subject, see the Appendix.

Chapter 2

What You'll Need to Train Your Dog

Before we start training, you'll need a few tools. Here's a list:

Collars	Chew toys and bones
Gates	Crates
Beds	Leashes

TYPES OF COLLARS

The Buckle Collar

This one's a staple. Your pet store might also refer to it as a tag collar. It fits around your dog's neck and carries her identification and inoculation tags. Whether your dog is two months or two years old, weighs two pounds or two hundred, find her a nice collar and attach those tags!

The Training Collars

You use a training collar only when your dog is on a leash. The only dogs exempt are toy breeds and puppies under sixteen weeks of age. 🐾 *Tip: You*

should avoid using training collars on puppies under sixteen weeks of age because their necks are still forming. Jerking or pulling on the collar would add too much stress to their developing trachea and could cause permanent damage. This in addition to the fact that infants dogs, like infant humans, can't even understand the concept of being corrected. Ahh . . . to be young again! Wait until your dog is sixteen weeks old before using a training collar.

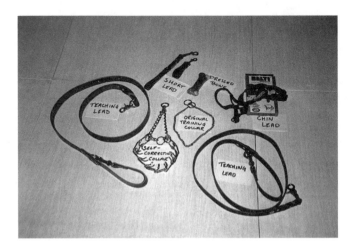

Some body-wear essentials.

There are three types of training collars; choosing one will depend on one thing . . . your dog! Find a collar that works for you and your dog from the following selection (try them all if you have to), and go with it. Good luck!

The "Original" Training Collar

I call it original because it's been around the longest. It has other names, too, such as a chain or choke collar, although used properly it should never choke your dog. Choking and restraint only aggravate problems. Most people don't know that it is the sound of the collar, not the restraint, which teaches. I know everyone would rather use it properly than hear their dog hacking during walks, but most people just don't know how to make the darn thing work.

Put the collar on correctly. Put on backwards, it will cause your dear doggy lots of discomfort. When the collar is fitted improperly, the links will catch in a vise-like hold around your dog's neck and do what the collar is not supposed to do: choke. Getting it on right, however, is a big challenge. It is one of the hardest lessons in my beginner class. Don't be discouraged if you get it wrong a time or two; just keep trying until you get it right.

First, decide which side you want your dog to walk on, left or right. You must be consistent, as dogs are easily confused. The left side is traditional, so I'll use it in my example.

1. Take one loop of the collar, and slide the chain slack through it.
2. Pretending you're on *Sesame Street*, create the letter "P" with the chain.
3. Holding it out, stand in front of your dog. Show her your creation.
4. With the "P" still facing in your direction, slide it over your dog's head as you praise her.

To check the result, slide the rings up behind her ears and stand at her left side. Grasp the moveable ring, and pull it towards your leg. Does it slide freely through the stationary loop (that's correct!), or does it bend over the stationary loop (try again)?

Mastering the zipper snap is the second step. Once again, it's the sound of the collar, not the restraint that teaches! Used properly, a quick snap (which sounds like a zipper) will correct your dog's impulse to disobey or lead. Here's an example of a typical situation:

Josie, my Collie mix and I, are walking in the park. Suddenly, we both notice Buster, her Bullmastiff friend, sniffing along with his owner, Tom, trailing behind. Buster immediately recognizes us and digs in to drag poor embarrassed Tom over for a visit. Though he must stop occasionally to re- lieve the nagging pressure around his neck, Buster doesn't comprehend that his coughing could be prevented if only he'd walk behind Tom. Once he's caught his breath, he's back on course.

THE HAND

When holding the leash, your hand is everything. Many people curl their fingers under the leash, which is incorrect. It encourages pulling forward and lifting up. Instead, hold the leash with your knuckles facing the sky and your thumb wrapped around the underside of the leash. Confused? Here's a little exercise: Hold your left arm straight out from your body. Pointing your thumb downward, lower your arm. As you do, curl your thumb under the leash and wrap your knuckles over the top! Ta da!

Josie, on the other hand, behaves a little differently. Though she squirms to be with her friend, she is quickly alerted to a zipping sound by her right ear. No vise hold, just a quick snap. A sound rather than a feeling. That coupled with the command "BACK" urges her to reconsider. She tries once more to pull ahead but is checked again with a zip! She chooses to wait for Buster behind my legs. Good choice, Josie.

"How did you do it?"

To master the zipper snap, you must practice the following exercise in a non-distracting environment:

1. Place the collar on the dog properly. Check it.
2. Attach the leash, slide the collar between the dog's ears, and position yourself on his left side.
3. Take the lead in your left hand.
4. Relaxing your arm in a straight position, hold the leash behind your thigh.
5. Here's the important part: Pretend there is a hinge in your elbow. Snap your elbow straight back behind you, as if you were trying to hit someone

standing in your shadow. Once you've snapped back, release the pressure immediately; this loosens the collar in preparation for the next snap. Remember, snapping backwards is a horizontal action. Since your dog walks in a horizontal line (he doesn't hop), it makes sense to him. Pulling him off the ground, on the other hand, makes the dog feel threatened and trapped, and instinctively he'll pull forward to get away. *Sound, not restraint. Don't forget.*

The "Self-Correcting" Collar

Yes, I know, it looks torturous. But it is perfectly humane, I promise, especially if you fall into the *I-can't-stop-choking-my-dog* category when using collar #1. This collar works on the quick external pinch-pain principle, which is far less damaging than a permanently crushed trachea.

The Germans developed this collar for many of their bull-necked breeds. I have found that it works wonders for dogs who are pain-insensitive or too powerful to persuade with a chain collar. Although it's officially termed a Prong Collar, I refer to it as "self-correcting" because it requires little strength to use. When you lock your arm into place, the collar pinches the dog; even the rowdiest of dogs will feel it and slow down. If you decide to give this collar a go, be sure to have someone with experience help you fit it on your dog and give you a quick lesson on its use. 🐾 *Tip: If you decide to try this collar, I need to warn you: Occasionally they pop off. To prevent an emergency, buy an oversized nylon slip collar and attach your leash to both collars when you are walking in an unconfined area.*

The "Chin" Lead

Once again, I have renamed a product. What the heck. It's more descriptive. Actually, this product comes in two forms. The pet stores sell a version known as a Halti. The other brand is called a Gentle Leader and is sold exclusively through veterinarians. They are esentially the same thing. I recommend this collar for clients struggling with an overexcited or headstrong dog. If you feel your dog is either, this may be the perfect solution. It eliminates the need to go into a choke battle and teaches your dog passively that you're in charge.

"It looks like a muzzle!"

I know. Trust me, it's not a muzzle. Dogs can eat, chew and play happily while sporting their chin lead. Taken a step further, it's probably the most humane way to handle a dog. It eliminates the need for collar corrections. Instead of teaching by applying negative pressure around the neck, it guides dogs gently by their head, like a halter on a horse.

"So how does this wonder collar work?"

It works on the "mommy" principle. When your dog was a pup, her mom would correct her by grasping her muzzle and shaking it. This communicated, "Hey wild one, settle down!" The chin lead has the same effect. When the collar is left on during play, the pressure on the nose discourages rowdiness and mouthing. By using the chin lead with the Teaching Lead or a short lead (coming up soon) when people visit, you can effectively curb jumping habits. Barking frenzies are also drastically reduced, as the pressure across the nose encourages a more submissive outlook. And last but not least, training is simplified as you guide your dog from one exercise to the next.

For those of you who can step beyond its muzzly appearance, the chin lead is a safe, effective, humane training tool that will give you a leg up in correcting negative behavior patterns. One more plus is that leading by the chin demands minimal physical strength, so nearly everyone can use it—kids, too!

"How long should you leave the chin lead on?"

This question can only be answered by one variable: your dog! If yours is relatively well-behaved, use it exclusively during training sessions. If she's the *mouthing-jumping-barking* maniac type, leave it on whenever you're around. Remove it at night or when you're away from the house.

SIZING YOUR CHIN LEAD AND EVALUATING YOUR DOG'S REACTION TO IT

A sizing scale is included with any chin lead you purchase. Once you've solved that problem, you must fit it properly around your dog's neck. If the chin lead is too loose, your dog will pull it off and may chew it. You want it to fit snugly about his ears and under his neck. You should be able to slip two fingers between the lead and your dog. (Halti owners: Once you fit the neck clasp, tie a knot with the remaining slack; this prevents the collar from coming loose.)

Initially, dogs don't like wearing a head collar. But they learn to tolerate it. So when you see your dog flopping about like a flounder, take a breath. Initial reactions are the most flamboyant. Once he realizes he can't get it off, he'll forget about it. Some take an hour; some, a day or two. If you find yourself wanting to give this collar a try, you may have to tolerate some resistance. Be patient.

CHOOSING AND USING GATES

Gates are optional, but if you have a puppy or young dog, you'll probably find them useful. They're great to close off a play area or to confine your dog if you are leaving the house (a crate is another option). Be sure to buy gates made of quality wood, metal or non-toxic vinyl mesh, and ones that are pressurized to fit your doorways. If you have breeds known for their athletic ability, look for extra-tall versions!

When considering where to confine your dog, keep these things in mind:

- Pick an area with linoleum or tiled floors in case of mishaps or accidents.
- Keep the area clear of loose objects that might be tempting to chew or swallow.
- Check electrical cords, and keep them out of reach. If they're on ground level, tape them to the wall securely; left alone, some dogs get mischievous.

Gates can also isolate dogs from off-limit areas and are handy for blocking dangerous stairways, ledges or porches.

"If I leave my dog confined when we're home, he goes nuts."

Your dog is suffering from isolation anxiety. A social creature, he doesn't understand why he's trapped away from you. Although at this point you'd fear his freedom, we'll be discussing how to remedy this situation to the satisfaction of you both later in the Teaching Lead section of this chapter.

Dogs also go nuts if they're confined when company arrives. Here, too, they're frustrated at being left out. Behind gates, most dogs are very excited: they jump, bark and get over-stimulated. Unfortunately, this behavior usually brings someone by to soothe them, which reinforces their wildings with, what else, attention. Another vicious cycle is created.

ABOUT BEDS

Not all dogs like beds. Some do, some don't. Your dog will tell you. She'll also let you know what kind of stuffing she prefers. Some are partial to beads. For others, only pseudo-lambskin or polyester fluff will do. If your dog likes one type, stick with it. If you need one bed for upstairs and one for downstairs, get identical beds. It may bore you, but dogs are habitual, and their learning is motivated by consistency.

CHEW TOYS AND BONES

Is your dog having difficulty differentiating his toys from other household objects? Once again, the consistency rule applies here. Take a look at how many toys are in his basket. More than one? I know, they were all special presents. But it's confusing, trust me. Too big a selection gives the dog the illusion that everything on the ground is a toy.

To make your expectations clearer, try this approach: Pick one or two favorites, and buy identical replicas to disperse around the house. 🐾 *Tip: Take your discarded toys and bones to a local animal shelter. They'll be appreciated more than you know. If you have a die-hard chewer, be sure to select a chew bone that will satisfy his gumming needs, avoiding soft toys that might feel like a couch cushion or fringed rug.*

CRATES

Crates are not mandatory in every situation, but they can be very helpful when used in moderation. They must be used humanely. Dogs can go nuts if left in a crate more than six consecutive hours day after day. Like us, they have active minds that demand companionship and stimulation. If you must leave your dog for long stretches, enclose her in a kitchen or bathroom, buy a fold-out dog pen from the pet store, and/or hire a dog walker to break up the monotony of the day. Given more space, she can stretch, play a little, and move about as she awaits your return.

LEFT ALONE

When leaving a dog alone, be sure to:
- Leave her in a dimly lit area (to encourage sleep).
- Leave the radio tuned to a classical music station (no hard rock).• Avoid grandiose departures,
- Avoid grandiose departures, which your dog interprets as, "Oh no, they're leaving me!!!"
- Stay cool during arrivals. Good manners start with you!
- Avoid corrections for anxiety behavior such as chewing or messing. You'll only be increasing her anxiety and the chance of the behavior happening again.

"What's the difference between a crate and a cage?"

Good question. They do look very similar. Crates, however, were not designed to cage dogs. Crates are supposed to replicate a denning area. Since dogs are instinctually drawn to a den, many of them find comfort in it. The problem with crates arises not from people who use them as sleeping or resting areas but from those who overconfine their dog hour after hour, day after day.

"What symptoms do overisolated dogs exhibit?"

Frenetic barking. Overly enthusiastic jumping. Excited nipping. And let's throw in destructive chewing for good measure. Poor creatures. It's not their fault. If they were human, they'd chew their nails, pull their hair out, and watch lots of soaps.

❧ *Note: I don't mean to insult anyone who uses crates a lot. Many books encourage crating when a dog cannot be watched all the time. It's not bad advice, as you don't want a destructive dog or untrained pup ravaging your house. For good-hearted people on the go, however, that means a lot of crate time for the dog left behind. This is what backfires. Alternatives are coming up shortly!*

"Are there any long-term effects of overcrating?

Yes, in some situations. Many of the dogs I've seen have developed what I call hyper-isolation anxiety. Too much isolation produces anxiety, and the anxiety produces hyper behavior. The dog actually acts clinically hyper when he's really not. Let me explain. A dog who's confined is not learning how to behave. When finally permitted some freedom, he has so much pent-up energy and so little understanding of good behavior that he starts tearing around the house like a lunatic. Yelling and chasing make matters worse, and so begins another vicious cycle in which the dog gets confined because no one knows how to handle the situation. UGH!

Crates can be very helpful training tools.

"How do we use it in moderation and not drive our dogs insane?"

Such good questions. Crates are great if used in the following situations:
- When you must leave your dog alone for less than six hours.
- During sleep time, for an unhousebroken or destructive pup or dog.
- As a feeding area for a distractible pup or dog.
- As a safe confinement in the car.

When crates are used properly, dogs feel secure and safe in them, just like their ancestors did in their dens. Crates also encourage good sleeping habits and discourage mischief and elimination. Happy dog, happy owner.

*"What's the alternative? Based on your suggestions, I
shouldn't crate my dog, but I'm away from home a lot and I
don't want to give my dog the run of the house."*

The alternative is to train with the Teaching Lead. It'll work wonders for
you and your dog. It's humane and fair, and makes rational sense to both
humans and dogs.

LET'S TALK LEASHES

The Teaching Lead

The Teaching Lead might look like any other leash, but once you understand
the concepts and the training theories behind it, it becomes a magical device.
Magical and manageable. It's leather, which adds extra leverage, so your
strength is increased. You'll feel more in control immediately. But it's the
holes and clips that makes the Teaching Lead truly unique (and fashionable,
to boot). I designed the leash to simplify a process I call Passive Control
Training.

Before we begin, let me tell you how it all got started . . . .

When I was just a pup (a teenager), I found this beautiful silvery white
Husky mix at a pound in Michigan. She was about six or seven months old
and had been rescued from the woods, sick with worms and caked with mud.
At the shelter, she hung back in her kennel, confused and shy. Everyone passed
her by. Everyone, that is, except me.

Though I asked the attendant many questions, all I can remember her
saying was: "She has a day to live." That was it. When I took the dog outside,
she peed quickly. Good, I thought, she's housebroken. "I'll take her," I said,
as a tear tumbled down my cheek.

I named her Kyia (which means "white" in Hawaiian), and she wasn't
housebroken. She also loved chewing wood—inside and out—was an avid

digger, peed every time a voice was raised or anyone bent to greet her, growled at her food dish and, in the height of play, jumped and nipped above the waist. OK, so who's perfect? But some training was definitely in order. I read some books. Crate, crate, crate, they instructed. It didn't resonate. How could confining her teach anything? But I bought one for the heck of it. She gave me a desperate look too similar to her first pitiful stare at the shelter. I folded up the crate and stuck it in the attic. Years later, I used it with a pup, but crates aren't for every dog, and it sure wasn't for Kyia.

Kyia

So what next? More books. *How to Be Your Dog's Best Friend*, by the Monks of New Skete, mentioned something about leading them around on a leash. A light bulb went off. That was the answer. I led her in the house and led her out. Whenever she sniffed the carpets, I chanted "Outside" as we raced for the backyard. Whenever she approached a tissue basket or wooden decoration, I pulled her back and said "No!" Being good at heart, she learned quickly. Within a few weeks, I stopped using the leash. She had learned the concepts of "Good Girl" and "No" and, as common sense would tell you, she strived for the positive.

So in those novice years, I discovered an alternative to the crate. This procedure felt more natural to me and to Kyia, and it worked. She was more secure and trained quickly. We bonded. It felt great. Years later, when I started my own training business, I didn't forget. As I listened to my clients complaining of their own guilty feelings about overisolation, I empathized and shared my story. I also told them about the Monks' book and two other books by authors Carol Lea Benjamin and Job Michael Evans that describe the process as "Umbilical Cording." Following my suggestions, my clients gave it a try, and it worked in nearly every situation. Year after year, I expanded on this process, creating ideas of my own until my techniques and teachings took on a personality all their own.

One day I was approached by a leathers man. He asked whether I needed any leashes. Another light bulb went off. With his help, I designed a leash to make my training suggestions easier to follow. The Teaching Lead was born.

Understanding my theories and the ways to use the lead to enhance them are what this book is all about. Soon, you'll understand how to use the Teaching Lead to do the following:
- Take the place of a crate when you're at home
- Teach basic obedience skills
- Gain control when walking outside
- Housebreak your dog
- Discourage nipping and jumping
- Encourage good chewing habits
- Calm your dog around company
- Further advanced obedience

🐾 *Tip: You can order the original patented version of the Teaching Lead through the order form in the back of the book, or you can create your own by using a durable six-foot leather lead and a double-headed clip from the hardware store. Attach one side of the clip to the end of the leash, and use the other end to secure the leash around your waist.*

The Teaching Lead teaches your dog to follow your lead!

The Teaching Lead has three applications: leading, anchoring and stationing. Understanding each is a must, as you'll be using them interchangeably. There will be days when you decide to lead more than station, and other days when that equation shifts. As long as you're humane and keep your dog close by, everybody will be happy.

A PREVIEW:

Leading is a technique of walking your dog that does not involve your hands. It is great for neighborhood strolls, afternoon jogs and household control. It is the process of using your leash to control your dear doggie both in the house, if necessary, and out. In addition to giving you instant control, this technique also teaches your dog, passively, who's in charge. No matter where you go, your dog must follow. If he gets into trouble, you're there for an immediate correction.

There is one twist, something that separates leading from an everyday walk in the park: Leading is done without hands. Instead of holding your leash, you'll wear it like a belt.

Skeptical? Here are two immediate benefits: 1) On the lead, you will make all the directional decisions. No matter where you go, your dog must follow. Passively, you communicate leadership. 2) A delinquent dog can't get into too much trouble when he's led. Dogs previously banned from certain areas in the house can be introduced in a more controlled fashion.

Anchoring is an approach to teaching your dog to lie calmly at your side while distracted.

Stationing teaches your dog to lie in a designated area on command. Although initally you'll need to reinforce your control with the Teaching Lead, eventually he'll go to his areas automatically.

"Wearing" your dog around the house may sound complicated, but you'll actually need to lead your dog full-time in the house only if she's too rambunctious to be trusted off-leash. Some of you may need to lead your dog only when company's around, or not at all. Read over the following three categories to see where you and your dog fit in:

1. Do tornado winds start to blow every time you let your dog loose in the house?

2. Home alone with you, she's a gem, but once kids come in or company rings the bell, her personality does a 180.
3. Your dog is Little Ms. Perfect. Mannerly in the home and polite around the guest. No problem.

Category 1. You need to use the Teaching Lead whenever you're around, either stationing or leading. Remember, it's not forever. For now, your dog must learn his manners from the bottom up.

Category 2. I suggest you practice leading periodically when you're home alone to get your dog used to the procedure. Use it full-time when you're expecting arrivals.

Category 3. We're all jealous. You need not worry about the Teaching Lead inside, but you'll find it handy for the obedience and off-lead training sections.

If you fall in category 1 or 2, don't worry. Using this technique is better than losing your sanity or your favorite shoes or confining your dog. It is definitely better than giving up. And it's only temporary. It's just until your dog learns to listen to you.

I know. It takes a few minutes to digest, but remember why you're doing all this: To teach your dog anything, you must be the leader. The boss. The apple of your dog's eye. Leading your dog communicates this passively. Where you go, he goes. If directional decisions are to be made, you make them. No arguing for control. No monkey business. There can be only one decision maker, one leader, and it must be you.

If your dog is a household maniac, leading enables you to keep him with you and under control. Instead of your blood pressure going up when you're correcting him, you can use leading to administer corrections quickly and encourage him through loving attention to adopt a calmer mind set.

Getting Started

Now, before we get started, we must agree on a few things:

1. You're a dog. Don't feel badly. So am I.
2. Being a dog, you need to have a secure place in the hierarchy.
3. Your place in the group is determined by your behavior.

4. You can decide to be a follower, bowing to your dog's every need and relinquishing any hope of behavior improvement or obedience, or . . .
5. You can decide to become a leader.

This is your moment . . . the big decision. If you want to be a follower, read no more. Burn the book. But! If you want to be the leader! Well, then read on. The rest of my book is dedicated to you.

The How-Tos of the Teaching Lead

1. First things first. Put your dog's training collar on, and attach the Teaching Lead to the collar clip.
2. Swing the lead around you like a belt, attaching the end clip to the appropriate waist hole.
3. Place the clip on one hip: either on the left hip if you want your dog to walk on the left, or on the right hip if you want your dog to walk on your right. Pick one side and be consistent. Dogs are habitual and easily confused. ❖ *Tip: Got kids who want (and are big enough) to help out? If the lead is too big, they can wear it like a banner. This also works well for expecting moms! With your dog secured to your side, safe from mischief and danger, take him everywhere.*

Leading

Remember, you don't even have to hold the leash. Just say, "Let's Go!" and you're off! As you are marching around, remember you're the leader. If you want to go in the living room but she'd rather check out the kitchen, it's the living room. Just go! Although she may pull or strain to have her way, just ignore her. Keep your head facing the living room, and walk on. Your dog will accept your decision and respect you more for making one.

Initially, many dogs strain to move in one direction or stop moving altogether when you first introduce them to leading. Granted, some are cooperative creatures who are just confused. For these fellows, I suggest kneeling down ahead of them and encouraging them forward. Pretty soon, they'll get the idea and be back on track. Some dogs, however, are less cooperative.

They're the tantrum throwers. The get-my-way-or-die doggies. When they walk on-lead, they imitate mules: Instead of walking, they just stop. Period. Won't move. Passive resistance. And if you look at them or pet them or pick them up, what are you encouraging? More resistance. It's that attention thing again. So for your own well-being, leave her down, stop petting, don't look. Just keep going, please. The sooner you do, the faster she'll give up her silent bid for control! I know, I hear you: "But she's dragging!" So practice on a linoleum floor, and use her buckle collar. Be strong. It's these little wars you must win. Think off-leash. Think of the slipper she chewed, or the shrub she excavated, or the neighbor she knocked over. If you can't convince her to walk with you, you'll never be able to persuade her to give up all her other darling habits. I know you can do it!

When they scoot ahead, change direction quickly and say "LET'S GO!" *Beth Wright.*

Taking a Break

We all need breaks. Just how many will depend on you and your dog. When considering this, your dog's age, size, behavior and temperament come into play. Older dogs can concentrate longer than puppies can. Leading is great exercise for smaller dogs, but bigger ones need play breaks to burn off their energy. Those with livelier temperaments also need more diversionary play activities than passive dogs do, who feel incredibly safe and calm next to your side.

Now for you. You'll also need a break. When you need a time-out from the dog belt, you have several choices:

a. Station your dog.
b. Go out and romp together.
c. Attach your dog to someone else.
d. Isolate your dog temporarily in an enclosure or crate.

Optimally, you want to keep your dog with somebody, so the first three choices would be best, but avoid feeling too guilty if you must isolate him for short periods of time. As long as the isolation is not extensive, your dog will survive. When reading over the stationing section, you may find that this option is as attractive as the crate. Since it encourages you to keep your dog nearby, he would probably opt for it.

"At what age should I begin leading?"

Young puppies enjoy short bouts, five to ten minutes, if they have been properly acclimated to the leash. (You can't do any leading, however, until they're leash-trained.) Puppies under sixteen weeks, however, have short attention spans and are very distractible. They continually cycle around their four need categories, which are the following:

Eating: When puppies are hungry, they must be fed. A consistent eating schedule is in order.

Sleeping: When puppies are tired, they sleep. You cannot drag them around when they're zonked.

Eliminating: When young puppies have to eliminate, they get very rambunctious and nippy. This is actually a good indicator that it's time to go out.

Exercising: When pups have energy, they need to release it! Wild'n-crazed energy spurts are normal, and they can have as many as four daily. The best thing for you to do at these times? Let your pup have freedom in an enclosed yard or kitchen while you climb a tree or stand on the counter tossing toys out randomly for your puppy to chase. No, I'm not kidding. Wild pups get nippy, and corrections only accentuate rough play (they think you're playing, too). It's better to wait until their engines cool before you attempt to reason with them.

"How long can I lead my dog around?"

That depends on a lot of things:

Age of dog. Young puppies cannot concentrate or sit still as long as older pups or dogs can.

Degree of habits. What category did you fall under in the "The Teaching Lead" section: 1, 2, or 3? If you're in category 1, you'll have to dedicate more to the initial stages than those from the other categories.

Your lifestyle. Are you around all day? You're very fortunate. You'll get to do more leading than those leaving the house for work. If you're gone all day, your time will be more limited. You'll need to devote some time to play and exercise, but when fun time's over, it's time to lead. Avoid isolating your dog when home, regardless of your lifestyle.

Your dog's personality. Sweet peas pick it up faster than the comedians; trust me, I've had both. But don't let that frustrate you if you've got a more active personality under your roof. They learn, too. They just take a little more persuading. The greater the challenge, the sweeter the victory!

"The whole thing sounds beautiful, but my dog thinks he's in a race every time I put him on the leash. How can I persuade him to walk without threatening my own safety?"

Here's my solution:

1. First, practice in a quiet room.
2. After placing the training collar on the dog and attaching him to your waist, let go of the leash with both hands.
3. Walk forward. The second your dog takes a step ahead of you, call out his name, pivot, and dart rapidly in the other direction. ❧ *Tip: The*

bigger the dog, the more rapid the dart. If you're practicing with a Chihuahua-sized dog, a strong baby step will do.

4. Whether or not you've got your dog's attention, praise him after you complete the turn.

5. In all likelihood, he'll race ahead again. So turn again. And again. And again.

6. Keep turning until the dog either alerts to his name or you collapse from dizziness. (Something I've done on numerous occasions!) Soon he'll be walking at your side!

Once you get him trained in the quiet room, go into a more distracted area. Each time your dog alerts to a distraction, call his name and dart. Keep practicing here until he stays by your side! Once that's perfected, venture out into the drive. Again, you might get too dizzy to stand straight, but keep at it.

Now that you're an expert of balance and coordination, use it on your walks. The next time your dog's radar picks up two gray tidbits playing in your neighbor's yard, call out his name and move in the opposite direction. Did the dog listen? If not, try again. And again. And keep turning until he puts your beckoning ahead of any distraction the environment might provide.

"Can everyone belt around?"

Everyone who can, should. However, use your good judgment. I wouldn't suggest hitching your three-your-old onto a Saint Bernard—or even to a Yorkshire Terrier—for that matter. Do not lead your dog around if you're physically impaired or very pregnant. But if older children and/or other adults want to take part in the house training, let them! Remember, dogs focus on a hierarchy, so it's best if everyone plays a part.

PREGNANT WOMEN AND CHILDREN can wear the leash like a sash, provided the dog is not large enough to pull them down.

YOUNG CHILDREN can lead the dog by holding a short lead. It's fun to hold and can be released immediately. My Car Lead doubles nicely for this activity! (Find out how to order it from the back of the book.)

Everyone who can lead, should.

"How can I get my dog to stop grabbing at the leash when I walk him?"

Dogs love this game! Such a fun activity! I know, fun for them, not for you. First you must put an end to all those tug-of-war games. They encourage struggles for control, including the battle of the leash. Next, rub Bitter Apple or Tabasco sauce on the lead. It has a vile taste that often discourages mouthing. If your dog loves that stuff (I had one who licked both right off my hand), then you must employ a tougher tactic. Each time your dog goes for the lead, snap it firmly *into her mouth*. Let me repeat that: Pull it *into* her mouth sharply, *not out*. I know that pulling the lead out is the more natural reaction; however, it only encourages a control struggle.

Maybe you'll understand better if I explain exactly why you want to pull the lead into her mouth and not out. It's a cause-and-effect reaction. You see, dogs view our hands as mouths. Since we're holding the leash, they want to hold it, too. For some dogs, it's a control issue; for others, it's more of a copy-cat reaction. When they do, however, the human reaction is to pull the lead out. Most dogs interpret this as fun, not discipline. And so they grab again. We pull the lead out. They grab. Grab-pull-grab-pull.

On the other hand, when the lead is pulled back into the mouth sharply, it doesn't feel so good. Though they may try it a couple more times, stern reactions and consistency will convince any dog that it's more comfortable to let the lead alone.

Into, not out. Don't forget.

"How come I feel guilty moving on when my dog drags behind me or stops to sniff?"

I don't know. Maybe you're the permissive type, concerned about your dog's feelings and needs and such. God bless you, but remember that your dog isn't human. She is more interested in figuring out who runs the show than in giving you brownie points for being nice.

"Do I have to lead my dog around forever?"

Of course not! Once your dog is responding to your verbal instructions and understands the rules (generally one to three weeks), you can start letting him drag the leash as you watch him meander around the house. If your dog behaves, praise him. Help him find his bones in each new space. After a few days of supervised freedom, try attaching a short lead. Slowly allow the dog more freedom, even when you can't be on his tail. Once he passes that test, he's a house-free dog. Congratulations to both of you!

🐾 *Note: Is your dog still out of control? You'll need to take it slower. Don't be discouraged, it's no big deal. I've had dogs who caught on in two weeks and others who took months. Everybody's different in the dog world, too. Be patient. Do some more leading and stationing before trying this experiment again.*

Anchoring

Suddenly the phone rings, or you have to work on the computer, or you're a kid and you've got to get some homework to do. What do you do with the dog? How do you teach the dog to quiet down when you're occupied? Off-leash, the dog would probably have you up rescuing a favorite shoe or the defrosting chicken. Unfortunately, it's just that attention thing again. But I have the answer. I call it anchoring.

When anchoring, give your dog just enough
freedom to lie next to you.

Whenever you're sitting down to answer the phone, speak to company, wait at the veterinarian's office, watch TV and so on, slide the end clip of the Teaching Lead around to your tailbone and anchor it under your backside. As the saying goes, sit on it! Give your dog just enough freedom to lie next to you. When she's settled, offer a favorite chew and a friendly scratch. In the beginning, however, expect a fuss. Your dog may whine, bark, paw or stare, which are all common attention-getting ploys. You must ignore her. Protests are a control thing; a dog who is used to directing your attention easily and giving you orders usually will be more resistant. It may take your dog fifteen minutes to settle down and chew her bone the first few times you try this exercise. This is normal, so be patient. But remember: when she finally does settle down, pet her. Look down upon her with the most loving eyes. Smile wide and look proud. If she hops up again, withdraw the attention quickly, but then return to soft loving caresses when she settles down.

"When I anchor my dog, he jumps on me. He's ninety-five pounds and a little hard to ignore. Do you have any other suggestions?"

Yes, I have three:

1. Fold your arms in front of your face. Tilt your head toward the sky, and don't look down until your dog is off. Repeat as often as necessary.

2. If the preceding correction has no influence, grasp the leash and snap it firmly down and back without looking or changing your body posture. No vocal correction is necessary. You're supposed to be ignoring your dog. It's the leash that's giving the correction. You step in to praise when your dog settles down at your feet. Your dog may try it again, so repeat your correction—perhaps a degree firmer.

3. If yours is a real die-hard jumper, sit on a very short leash so that the jump itself will bring about a correction. Release some slack when the dog decides to lie down.

"When I anchor my dog, she lies down but immediately twists around to lay on my feet. Is this acceptable?"

Great question. No, it's not. Ideally, she should be laying next to your left side. Everytime she twists forward, shift her back with your hands. (And don't give her eye contact until she's laying in the right space!) You may need to do this several times, but she'll comply eventually. Just be persistent.

THE STORY OF KIBBLES

Kibbles is a fun-loving year-and-a-half-old Cocker–Cavalier King Charles Spaniel cross rescued from the shelter by a loving family. Having spent a third of his life without a family, Kibbles can hardly sit still. There is even a pond in the back yard and two dog friends who stop by each afternoon to play! Heaven or what? Kibbles is so busy taking it all in, however, that he doesn't pay attention to bathroom habits. Wherever will do: upstairs playing dress-up with the girls, in the kitchen on a break from his nightly begging rituals, out on the deck if there's no incentive to leave the house, or on the grass if the mood strikes him. He's not picky. He's not marking. He's not lazy. He's just clueless!

From the moment I met Kibbles, I was charmed by his sweet and eager personality. Before ten minutes had passed, however, he trotted out on the deck, peed quickly, and ran back inside for some more attention. No remorse. No guilt. No understanding. This happens to a lot of shelter dogs. They think they can pee anywhere. Can you blame them? Well, it was time for the Teaching Lead. After showing everyone (including the girls, who wore the lead like a beauty sash) how to lead Kibbles, I further explained housetraining techniques. Until Kibbles was cooperating, he was to be led or stationed. Surprisingly, Kibbles took to the leading like a shadow to the dark and happily followed whoever was in charge. It was like he had been waiting for a good leader all his life! Within just a few weeks, Kibbles had regained his freedom in the house and had learned to jingle some bells by the door in case his owners forgot a walking!

Stationing

Stations are areas you give your dog in every room you permit her to be in. They're her spots. Just like we humans feel more comfortable knowing our place in a room, so do dogs.

Eventually, you'll be able to send your dog to any area in any situation by using a command like SETTLE DOWN. I realize that for some of you this might sound like a fantasy, but trust me, it'll happen. The key word is "eventually." First you must do some training.

Here's a short instruction course in stationing:

PICK YOUR AREAS Select an area in each room where your well-mannered dog will be permitted. Make sure it's away from heavy-traffic areas and electrical outlets. In addition, make sure each area is near enough to something onto which you can initially secure the lead. This will be your dog's space, and eventually she'll go there automatically, but for now you must keep her leashed.

🐾 *Note: You can have two stations or twenty, it's up to you. You can also have a car station and outdoor stations (great for barbecues and badminton games).*

Here are some ideas.

Family Room: Since everyone wants to pet the dog while watching TV or playing Nintendo, you can create this station near the couch.

Dining Room: Unless you like dog slobber with your ketchup, you can create this station across the room so that your dog won't be tempted to disturb you. This one really impresses house guests and in-laws!

The Kitchen: Unless you have a huge kitchen, you might want to station your dog outside the kitchen door. This way, she can watch all the preparations without getting underfoot.

Greeting Area or Front Hall: Dogs tend to get overexcited during arrivals. Left free, their enthusiasm can get in the way and is usually reinforced,

**Give your dog stations in every room in which
he'll be permitted.**

unintentionally, by (what else?) attention. To avoid such hysterics and provide a better alternative, create a station in a corner of the greeting area. When the doorbell rings, instruct your dog to go to her place, secure her, give her a special toy, and ignore her until she pipes down. The best of all possibilities is involvement without interference!

Bedrooms: Some of you may refuse the idea, but the truth of the matter is that your dog will feel safer and act a lot calmer *during the day* if she's kept with someone at night. This is especially true for those dogs left during the working hours. If your dog is older than four months and still needs confinement, station him at night in your bedroom.

❧ *Note: Are some of you neat freaks who wouldn't mind the dog if it weren't for all the hair, smell and dirt? Well, I can relate. You might see a lot of paws in my house, but I do like a clean and pleasant-smelling home. Here's my suggestion. In the bedroom, use a white sheet as a bedding cover. Spread it out so that your dog will have to lie on it; then toss it in every wash. You'll be happy and free of dog odor, and your dog will be delighted to have a place by your bedside.*

Dogs are much happier sleeping near you at night.

Office: Some of you might be lucky enough to take your dog to work if he'd only behave. Now you've got a green light. Pick a spot by your desk, decorate it just like home, and away you go!

Outside: If you're into gardening or you have kids who like to shoot hoops in the driveway and you'd be all for including the dog if he'd just calm down, you can help out by creating nearby stations.

Car: It's safest to confine your dog while driving. It protects them like a seat belt protects you. Crates can be cumbersome, so I created a method of car stationing, which is described in more detail later in this chapter.

DECORATE STATIONS   Create a familiar theme at each station. Similar bedding and chew bones will help your dog learn faster.

KEEP YOUR DOG CLOSE   Stationing enables you to keep your dog with you. If you're moving around the house, don't forget to move your dog around with you.

SECURE YOUR DOG NEAR YOU   When you station your dog, give her just enough room to lie comfortably (about three feet). Given too much leeway, dogs may pace, bark or (worse) eliminate. There are two ways to organize your stations:

- On the Teaching Lead, you'll notice a station hole next to the dog clip. When stationing, attach the end clip to the station hole. If you're attaching the clip to a high object, you might need to attach the end clip to a waist hole to give your dog adequate moving space.
- Once you've predetermined your stations, attach old leashes or create lines out of ropes and clips. The lines can be attached to fixtures and left until your dog is responding on her own.

SHOW YOUR DOG THE STATION   The first time you secure your dog, hang around. Sit down and scratch her ears. Show her the bone. When she's content, say "WAIT" as you walk away for no more than fifteen seconds. If you come back to a hyped dog, ignore her until she quiets down. Pet a calm dog, you get a calm dog. Increase your departures steadily. She may fuss a bit, but your preliminary steps will ensure her of your return.

GIVE YOUR DOG THE COMMAND   Each time you send your dog to a station, say "SETTLE DOWN" and point to the bed. She won't have a clue for

PLAYING WITH YOUR DOG

Certain games encourage interaction, which is good. Others encourage confrontation, which is not so good.

Good Games

Snoopy Soccer: I play this game with an empty plastic soda bottle or milk jug, removing both the paper and the cap. A regulation ball will also do the trick. The rules for this game: no hands! This one is great for kids and dogs because it keeps the kids standing up while the dog is focused on the ground. (Once the plastic container is punctured, discard it.)

Ricochet Rover: This version of fetch is simple. You throw, the dog retrieves. If you have a dog who will release the ball to you immediately, then this is the game for you. If your dog finds it more amusing to play keep-away, however, than you must teach the release (instructions in Chapter 4) before you play, or play with several balls to avoid confrontation.

Hide and Seek: Most dogs don't like to lose sight of their owners. When your dog is sniffing around on her Flexi-leash or in an enclosed area, call out her name and encourage her focus. When she looks up, race away and hide behind something (tree, house corner, etc.). When she finds you, give her a big hug!

Fishing for Fido: I have a lot of fun with this one. Find a stick. This is your "fishing rod." The bait will be a squeak toy. Pick out a favorite, and tie it to the stick with a four-foot piece of string. Now, when your dog is really hyped, you can wave your rod around and help her burn off all that excess energy! Don't tease her though; let her catch the bait from time to time. Keep the game fun!

Here I am, fishing for Lucy.

Bad Games

Tug-of-War: This game makes dogs think the struggle for leadership is still on. It's very confrontational and bad if they win. What an ego booster! They soon start challenging you for the leash, biting down harder during play and even trying to rip the shirt from your back!

Rough Housing: Another confrontational event. Some dogs don't take it too seriously. Others do. They think it's a challenge to their identity. They may growl or mouth too excessively. Keep pushing them and they'll start to snap, even when you're not playing. I think it's best to avoid wrestling altogether.

Teasing: Seems pretty obvious. You might need to remind the kids. Sometimes, kids tease the dogs to get attention. Sound familiar? If you see this happening, try to pay more attention when your children are interacting peacefully, and walk out of the room when the teasing begins. Often, when you leave, they stop.

a while, but eventually it'll click. You'll be amazed when she starts doing it herself. Dogs, like people, are more cooperative when they understand what you want.

GIVE YOUR DOG ATTENTION   As we've discovered, the unsupervised dog often gets attention for being naughty. Poor thing, she can't help herself. On the other hand, a stationed dog doesn't have a lot of room to act up. Sure she may bark, but if you ignore that it'll go away. (For truly incessant barkers, other alternatives are discussed in Chapter 6.) She might roll around a bit and act kooky, but you can ignore that, too. How bad can she be with only a three-foot area, a blanket and a favorite chew? Stationing encourages one thing: good behavior. So whenever your dog lies down to rest or chew, you can reinforce her with you know what . . . ATTENTION! Don't get too wild. Just go over (or send the kids), and happily give her some love and pats. Tell her she's a gem. You're so proud. You're so glad you found her.

GIVE YOUR DOG A BREAK   You can't station a dog all day long. When it's time for a break, you can either do some leading or have free play in the kitchen or an outside enclosure.

"How long can I leave my dog stationed?"

The amount of time you can station a dog depends on (you guessed it!) your dog. Age and temperament are paramount. Add time of day and weather to the equation. Puppies under twelve weeks can have stations; they just can't be attached to them. Older puppies and dogs can be attached, but, as common sense would dictate, young dogs need more breaks than older ones do. Time of day is also a factor. Is it nap time? You can expect more peace and quiet than if you station during an energy peak. In addition, rainy days usually mean less exercise, making it tough for active dogs to sit still for too long.

"What if I have nothing to station my dog to?"

You can get some eye hooks from the hardware store and screw them into a wall or the underside of a cabinet.

"What if my dog won't stop barking?"

If you've tried ignoring her for ten minutes and she won't give up, you'll need to graduate to a more severe measure. Here are a few suggestions:

- Buy ear plugs and wait it out. No joke.
- Get a fancy long-distance water gun (the kids call it a super soaker), and indiscreetly spray her while you firmly say "SHHH!" She must not know where the water is coming from. Offer praise and attention once she calms down!
- If you've got a splitting headache, the baby's crying, and your spouse is threatening divorce, very calmly remove your dog from the station. The key rule still applies: No eye contact. Look disappointed as you lead your dog from the station, and ignore her for fifteen minutes.

"What if my dog panics?"

It's common for young puppies to panic, so if that's the case, ease up on your routine. If your dog is older, you must determine whether the reaction is really panic or simply a persuasive protest. Ignore the protest. If she's truly panicked, try to figure out why. Is she over-sensitive to weather changes or loud noises? Is she just needing a good romp and can't sit still? Did you feed her her last meal? Are the kids safe? Go down your checklist. If it all pans out and she's still antsy, wait for her to take a breath, and go and sit with her. Encourage bone chewing, leaving her side only when she's sleeping. Pretty soon, she'll get over it, whatever it is.

"What if my dog chews his Teaching Lead?"

If you suspect your dog will chew his lead, avoid using your Teaching Lead to station him until he's learned better manners. Tie up old nylon leashes or ropes to the predetermined station areas (soaking them ahead of time with Bitter Apple liquid or your own concoction of Tabasco sauce). If all else fails, get a chain lead to station him temporarily until he gives up the idea.

"Do I have to leash my dog forever?"

Of course not! Some dogs catch onto the SETTLE DOWN command so quickly they're eagerly participating by the end of the second week. Others take longer, but what's the rush? Whether it takes a couple of weeks or months, once your dog learns this little trick, it lasts a lifetime. Mine were initially more cooperative when no one was around, but when I invited friends in, it was not such a pretty picture. So for a while, I stationed when company was around. No biggy. Since my dogs are just like yours, you'll probably find yourself leaning on the Teaching Lead from time to time, too.

The Car Lead

Driving is a job in itself! Avoid being preoccupied with your dog while doing it, as it's a safety hazard for both of you—not to mention for other motorists. Letting your dog ride in your lap or hang his body halfway out the window may seem cool, but it's really not. Maybe I've witnessed too many accidents, but to me, cars aren't toys and your dog is too precious to lose in a fender bender. Here's my safety rule: Confine your dog while driving. There are car gates, crates, harness belts and—my little invention—the Car Lead.

Car gates confine dogs to a back area. I find them bothersome in my station wagon because it limits what I can transport, but if you go that way, buy the best-quality gate you can find. When I was in college at Michigan State University, I bought a cheap gate to confine my husky-mix Kyia in my station wagon. We were on our way home to New York when the thing collapsed. Poor Kyia. Such a sweet pea, she was sure she had caused the crash and was remorseful the rest of the trip home. Moral of story? If you're going to buy a gate, buy the best!

Crates are cumbersome but can also be used to secure your dog. Another alternative is a harness-type seat belt. This is a great concept, but difficult to use. Dogs aren't jazzed about sitting still as you clip them in, and, let's face it, who's got the time?

There is, however, a great alternative. I invented and patented it, and I call it the Car Lead. Here's what it looks like, and here's how it works:

1. The handle of the Car Lead fastens onto a seat belt. It can be left in the car permanently.
2. Now your dog has a car station. Decorate it with a blanket and a toy!
3. Bring her to the car; then say "GO TO YOUR SPOT" as you point to the area. Offer a treat for cooperation.
4. Hook her up on the buckle collar (not a training collar), and ignore all initial protests. Praise her when she's calm.

The Car Lead protects dogs like a seat belt protects people. It's quick and easy to use, and your dog will feel more secure and calm knowing her place. You're both ensured of a safe arrival.

BAILEY THE BEAGLE

Bailey is an adorable eight-month-old Beagle. Although he is given a high-quality dog food (which he eats with gusto), he hangs around the kitchen table, looking soulful and starved. This technique usually pays off with a few pats and an occasional tidbit, although both his owners would prefer that he lie down in the corner. Bailey also enjoys begging during formal dinner parties. His owners would like to take him along when they visit family and friends, but Bailey's food manners have placed him on the "B" list for most social affairs.

Bailey as the welcome party guest.

When I met Bailey, I discovered a very happy fellow who thought begging was just the right thing to do. How could something that resulted in attention and treats be wrong? I suggested that his owners create a station in the kitchen at least ten feet from the table. As I predicted, Bailey barked during the first few meals, but his determined owners ignored him. Soon after, he began to settle down and chew his bone. Within a month, he was staying in his area off-leash. The Teaching Lead has helped Bailey make a successful transition from social outcast to welcome guest.

The Short Lead

How short your Short Lead should be depends on the size of your dog. A Short Lead should not be more than eight inches long; for small dogs, one inch will do. My Car Lead doubles nicely for bigger dogs. If you've got a half-pint, buy a key chain and use that.

We'll be using this handy little device for two things: encouraging manners and training off-leash. Here's the theory behind both:

Encouraging mannerly behavior: A lot of clients complain that their dog behaves like a saint on the Teaching Lead, but take it off . . . the old derelict emerges. Off-leash owners get trapped into chasing the naughty dog, and what is chasing? It's attention! A short leash can serve as a nice transition from the Teaching Lead to full-fledged freedom. Wearing it reminds the dog that you're still watching, and having it on gives you something to grasp and correct if things get out of hand.

Car Leads keep dogs safe. They can be left in
place for quick and easy use.

Off-lead training: When you do off-leash work, you can use the Short Lead as a reminder. In addition, it's something you can grab graciously if your dog slips up.

The Flexi-Leash

Flexi-Leashes are fun, period. The longer, the better. To begin with, they're great for exercising. Your dog can run like mad while you stand there reading the morning news. And if you feel like exercising, too, all the better. You can quadruple your dog's workout. When we progress to off-leash work, the Flexi will be a staple. Its tidy design works like a fishing reel, and although using the leash requires some coordination, once you've mastered the technique, you won't be able to live without this leash.

The Flexi-Leash can be dangerous, however; its high-tech design takes some getting use to. Practice in isolated areas until you've got the system down pat.

If you're out with other people, watch their legs. Most dogs get a little nutty when finally given some freedom to run. If a person gets sandwiched between you and your dashing dog, OUCH! They're in for a wicked rope burn! It's best to keep playtimes private.

Some dogs love to chew their Flexi. After all, the exercise and freedom are so exciting! Soaking the cord in Bitter Apple liquid overnight can be a good deterrent. If this is ineffective, try snapping the cord into your dog's mouth.

If the worst happens and the cord is severed, get a Phillips head screw driver, open up the box, and sew the cord back together. It takes ten minutes and is cheaper than buying a new one.

Long Lines

We'll use long lines in Chapter 6, when we get into more off-leash stuff. I don't want to overwhelm you now with the details, but if you're really organized and optimistic, you can create these lines according to my specifications and put them aside for later. There are three types of long lines:

1. *The Tree Line:* You'll tie this one onto a tree. More later. For now, either buy a thirty-foot line or create one with a clothesline and a clip.
2. *The Drag Line:* Buy or make a twenty-five-foot line.
3. *The House Line:* Buy or create a ten-foot line.

Now that you're all equipped, it's on to some more adventurous stuff!

Chapter 3

Starting Off on the Right Paw

Your mother was right, first impressions count! Starting off on the right paw is what will set the stage for all your future goals. Want your off-leash dog to respond to a "COME?" Then pay close attention to the foundation you lay. If you're inconsistent with the basics, then guess what? Your dog will never take you seriously with the more advanced stuff. It's not as difficult as it sounds. Really. I've outlined this chapter to make it as simple, interesting and fun as possible. Let's begin!

In this chapter, we'll cover:

The Conversational Technique
The Magic Seven
Universal Discipline
The Power of Praise

THE CONVERSATIONAL TECHNIQUE

When I was I kid, I remember taking a dog-training class with an instructor who told everyone to practice twice a day for fifteen minutes. This was not unusual or bad advice, and back when I was a kid, it was very do–able. Now that I'm a grown up, however, I can hardly find two minutes in my day to brush my teeth. I found myself in the same predicament my clients complain of: new dog or old problems, who can find the time to devote to training?

I'll tell you what I do now that I'm grown up. I use my training commands conversationally throughout the day: "SIT" before petting him or giving him treats, "EXCUSE ME" when I've got a dog underfoot, "LET'S GO" to change direction, and "NO" for the naughty stuff.

By using specific commands consistently, your dog will start picking up on what you want and (like magic) start cooperating. Without taking time out of your day, you can teach your dog "The Magic Seven."

THE MAGIC SEVEN

The magic seven are your start-up commands. Though we'll look at them one at a time, you should use them all throughout your day. Yes, your dog can learn seven at once if you're consistent. Here they are!

> SIT
> BUDDY (or whatever your dog's name is), LET'S GO
> EXCUSE ME
> BUDDY
> WAIT and OK
> NO
> SETTLE DOWN

The biggest motivating factor in training is you. To be a good teacher, you need to be consistent, clear and compassionate.

Be consistent. Use the same commands in each appropriate situation, and encourage everyone involved with your dog to do the same. If two people have different expectations, your dog won't know who to believe. Be clear in your communication. Use Doglish, not English, and stand tall and over-enunciate. And last, but not least, be compassionate. Praise a lot.

SIT

This command is one of my favorites. Why? Because once you start using it consistently, your dog will start doing it automatically. Consistently-automatically. It's a wonderful thing. To teach this command, use it before:

- dinner
- treats
- a toy or bone toss
- petting
- greetings
- letting your dog outside, inside, down the stairs or out of the car

Make SIT a user-friendly command.

You can make this command so user-friendly that your dog will actually look forward to hearing it. No kidding! He'll end up liking it so much he'll start responding before you get the word out of your mouth. Sound like a

fantasy? Well, it's not, but it does require the proper training approach. Here are the rules:

1. Be consistent! If you ask for a sit, get a sit. No empty commands!

2. Say it once. Your dog understand sounds, not words. "SIT-SIT-SIT" sounds different than "SIT."

3. Stand tall when you give the command. If you asked me to do something while you were bending over, I'd think you had lost something rather than respect your call. Your dog might wonder the same or view your posture as indecisive. Stand tall, proud leader.

4. If your dog doesn't listen, don't sweat. Praise and position him. Yes, I said "praise." Even if he doesn't listen. Initially, it is important to create a friendly feeling toward new commands. For now, give the command once, then praise as you position.

It's a motivational approach. It's positive. Your dog will want to get involved. And he'll equate sitting with getting attention. Finally, that attention equation is working in your favor! *Tip: Hey Parents and Kids: If you belong to a big family, you'll have to help your dog out. Since everybody sounds different, life can get pretty confusing. When you give the commands, over-enunciate your syllables. Instead of using a blah "SIT," make the command come to life by exaggerating the "T" sound: "SITTT!" Everyone will sound more alike, and the dog will love the animation and respond better to the whole family!*

BUDDY, LET'S GO!

This command is a real beauty. Another favorite. It communicates leadership passively without thought or effort. And, on top of that, it's relatively easy to master!

First, practice inside while leading your dog. No hands allowed; just belt on the Teaching Lead, let go and move. That's the gist of it. Where you go, your dog goes: dusting, phoning, laundering, whatever. . . . Take-home message: Dog follows leader. (That's you!) Whenever you change direction, say "LET'S GO." And when you say it, do it. Go. Don't check to see whether your dog approves. Just go. You're teaching your dog that when he hears this command he must obey.

I know, in the beginning some dogs can be a handful. If yours is the racing-ahead type, change direction every time he starts to bolt. If he starts running, you say "LET'S GO" and pivot in the opposite direction. If he ignores you, you tug on the lead. Too bad, he'll pay more attention the next time. You're the leader. The boss. Pretty soon he'll notice that when you say it, you mean it.

Are any of you experiencing the opposite? Instead of pulling, your dog's not moving. Laying down on the job. Won't budge. Unfortunately, he's communicating the same thing: *I, dog, create the pace.* Don't buy into this! If you do, you're trashing all your training efforts. The leash is where it all begins. If you can't control the rhythm on the leash, forget about controlling him off of it. I know it's hard, but you must ignore him. Don't look back—no soothing—just dig those heels in and keep going! Yes, you may have to drag him a bit, but don't look back! He'll get up, and when he does, praise him.

Here's a fun exercise for you! Take a look at these everyday situations and decide on the best option:

Situation "LET'S GO" #1

It's hot, you're sitting on the couch watching a re-run of *Star Trek*, your dog's around your waist, and suddenly you're craving mint chocolate chip ice cream. After five minutes of deliberation, you decide to head for the freezer, but as you get up, your Maltese, Max, has another idea. He hears the neighborhood children outside and wants to go check out the fun. You're still thinking ice cream, though. He's pulling you right; you're wanting to go left. Which of the following three actions should you take?

a) Immediately take Max out to see the kids?

b) Pet him as you try to explain the situation, bribing him with a cone if he'll only cooperate?

c) March confidently into the kitchen, saying "LET'S GO," with dear doggy in tow until he realizes that your way is the only way?

Did you guess (c)? Yeah!!! The leader dog enforces his direction. Options (a) or (b) would have communicated Max's responsibility for you!

Did you miss that one? Here's another chance:

Situation "LET'S GO" #2

You're outside walking Sierra, your Samoyed. For a few moments, all is calm. A nice walk. But suddenly another dog appears on the opposite side of the street. Sierra's a friendly gal and immediately wants to head over for a visit. She begins pulling you across the street. What should you do?

a) Go with Sierra?
b) Pet Sierra, telling her to settle down?
c) Snap Sierra's chain, say "LET'S GO," and continue walking without hesitation?

Did you pick (c)? Yeah! Sierra needs to understand that she can't investigate every dog or person she sees. The other options support her leadership, in addition to communicating a mutual curiosity. Off-leash, she'd follow her impulses and be in serious danger from oncoming cars.

"Should my dog walk on one side?"

Yes. Your dog is a habitual creature. If you want him on the left, keep him to the left; if you want him on the right, keep him to the right. In the beginning, he may get confused and wander back and forth from side to side. When he does, say "EXCUSE ME" and shift him over.

"It sounds mean. Can't we ever go in their direction?"

Not when you're starting out. When you begin training, you're communicating leadership. If you're inconsistent, your dog will develop a kind of *if-I'm-in-the-mood attitude.* "COME!" *Ah—in a minute.* "SIT." *No thanks, I'm busy. Maybe later.*

❧ *Note: If you want to give your dog some freedom to explore, buy a Flexi-Lead. When he's back on the Teaching Lead, however, more civilized manners are in order.*

"LET'S GO" communicates one thing and one thing only: You're the leader! Wherever you go, your dog must follow. Initially, it may not be his idea of fun, but he'll like your praise for this forced cooperation and soon be tagging along for the enjoyment! You leader you. . . .

EXCUSE ME!

This command carries the same meaning for dogs as it does humans. For dogs, however, it has a little more to do with hierarchy and leadership than with common courtesy. In dogland, it's a respect thing. Subordinates naturally watch out for their leaders.

Now ask yourself, how often does your dog *naturally* watch out for you? How often does she automatically get up and move aside when you pass through? Once in a while? Never, perhaps? Rule is, from now on, if your dog is in your way, say "EXCUSE ME" and move her to one side. No stepping over. No walking around. No changing direction. If she won't move, shimmy your feet beneath her or nudge her aside with your knees. Don't re-navigate an inch.

Here are some other situations in which the EXCUSE ME command applies:

The Leaners: Is your dog a leaner? I'm not talking about the occasional-lean-in-for-a-scratch fellows. I'm talking about the big timers—two pounds or 200, you'd know who they are. It's obvious. They'll sit in front of you and lean on your legs. Whether you're talking with someone, on the phone, or pausing to catch a breath, they consider the opportunity golden for a body press.

What's wrong with leaning? you ask. Isn't it affectionate? Sometimes. But when a dog starts overdoing it, it has more to do with dominance in the hierarchy. Consider yourself and someone close to you. Close contact is desirable at times, but if they have their arm around you every second, it would be annoying and inappropriate. And what would you say to them? The same thing I'm encouraging you to say to your dog . . ."EXCUSE ME!"

The Herders: The herders are just as obvious. It's impossible to walk a straight line with these fellows. They like to get in front and lean in for a directional change. No go. Stay on course. And if you run into them . . . "EXCUSE ME!"

EXCUUUZZE ME!

The Blockers: These guys are very blatant about their intentions. They block the TV and stairways, and are known to position themselves in between loved ones when affection is being offered. Sound familiar? These guys are taking the comedy thing a step too far. Out of the way chum . . . "EXCUSE ME!"

Here are some more situations to play around with. Good luck!

Situation "EXCUSE ME" #1

You're sitting in your favorite lounge, speaking to a close friend on the phone, dog around your waist. When you go to hang up the phone, you notice Quigley, your Golden Retriever, laying right in your pathway. Should you:

a) Step over him?
b) Bend to pet him, then step over him?
c) Say "EXCUSE ME" first and then pet him if you're in the mood?

Did you answer (c)? If you're ever unsure, pick (c). Seriously, doing anything but what's described in (c) would be subservient. You'd be communicating that your dog's in charge. Asking your dog to move may not seem like a big deal to you, but it communicates a lot to him.

Situation "EXCUSE ME" #2

Rascal, your big Rotweiller, notices you on the telephone. Immediately he seizes the opportunity to come over for a scratch. You brace yourself for the lean. As expected, he presses up against your thighs and looks up with his soulful expression. Do you:

a) Pet him as you take a few steps back?

b) Look down smiling and signaling that you'll be one more minute on the phone?

c) Thrust him away from your body with your knees and say "EXCUSE ME," repeating this until Rascal holds his own space?

You guessed it, (c). You're catching onto this leadership thing.

"Will this apply when my dog is constantly pressing her toys against me and putting them in my lap?"

A big Steve Martin "EXCUUUZZE MEE!" Only kidding. But it does fall under this category. First of all, don't pay any attention. No eye contact. No toy holding, tug-of-war, fond scratch beneath the ears until you get too fed up and start yelling. None of that. Simply knee her away as you say "EXCUSE ME." Don't look at her; just say it. I had a dog I had to nudge away thirty-two times. What a nightmare. But she caught on, and so will yours. Just be patient. When she gives up and lays down to chew, pet her calmly.

"Will this command help when my dog crosses in front or behind me during a walk?"

Yes. Grab the leash, and haul him over to the appropriate side as you say "EXCUSE ME." Also use this command if your dog leans on you when you stop.

🐾 *Note: If your dog is overtly dominant, growling or looking at you sideways when asked to move, avoid this exercise. Get professional help immediately. You've got an aggressive dog, and the sooner you address the problem, the better chance you'll have of remedying it. Push this character aside and he may bite.*

BUDDY

The object is to get your dog alerting to his name, regardless of the distractions. It's the first step in the off-leash COME command exercise. You call, he checks in. Big goal.

1. Go into a quiet room, and instruct "SIT."
2. Fold the leash into one hand, and hold it loosely above his head.
3. Pivot directly in front of your dog, your toes facing his paws.
4. Stand extra tall. The Peacock Position.
5. As you call out his name, "BUDDY!", bring the free index finger from his eyes to yours.
6. Cluck. Yes, cluck to encourage focus.
7. When he looks up, stare back until he breaks the stare.

🐾 *Note: If he refuses to look or just gives you a quick glance, snap the leash and say "NO." Standing tall, repeat the preceding steps. Try some fancier clucks. Avoid getting mad or frustrated as it only makes you look foolish.*

If you're handling a pup, drop the "NO" correction. If your pup's being uncooperative, try holding his head steady to meet your eyes.

Use your dog's name to encourage eye
contact. *Sally Sarsfield.*

🐾 *Note: Uplift: If you have a small breed or little pup, practice this exercise on a stair or table, or kneel in front of her. Continue to keep your back straight, and use your finger to draw a line from her eyes to yours.*

You will begin to notice that when you call, your dog looks up. Try it before mealtime. Call out his name before offering a treat. Try a quick name-check before tossing a ball. He'll love it. You say "BUDDY!" His eyes say "YES BOSS!" The start of a beautiful relationship.

"My dog won't look up at me for anything."

She's not taking you very seriously. Are you standing tall? Speaking in a commanding tone? Relaxed? If so, when she ignores you, check the lead and tell her "NO."

"My dog jumps up and barks when I stare at him."

He thinks you're his playmate. Knowing that, prepare to snap him aside and say "NO" when he starts to get excited.

"My dog won't break the stare."

Oh, yes she will. Keep staring. If she won't let up, distract her by stamping your foot.

"My dog growls at me."

Get help. Avoid this exercise. You've got a potential aggression problem.

WAIT and OK

A quick show of hands, please. How many of you have dogs who would plow you over if you got between them, the doorway and the great outdoors; have skillfully mastered the art of door dashing as you're greeting company; jump maniacally out of or into the car; haul you into every new experience or situation with the power of a charging bull?

Were your hands up for any or all of these situations? Embarrassed? Guess what? You're encouraging each situation by allowing such chaos. It's time to take control.

First you must teach your dog these commands: WAIT (stop and focus) and OK (it's all right to move). It's permission training. A self-control thing. Here's how:
1. Pick any threshold in your home.
2. Holding your dog to your side, walk to this area.
3. Stop abruptly as you reach the threshold, and say "WAIT."
4. If she bolts anyway, say "NO!" as you pull her back. Repeat "WAIT."

5. Repeat the pullback as often as necessary until she pauses.
6. Encourage her to look at you by saying her name or making some clucking sounds.
7. Once she's checked in, say "OK" as you lead her through. Feet ahead of paws.

**Make sure you always lead your dog
out the door.**

Now you're ready for the big time! Go to your main entrance. Prepare yourself as described previously, holding the leash back behind your body. Command "WAIT" just before you open the door. If your dog bolts, be ready. Snap her back behind your feet, and say "NO!" Repeat "WAIT." When she does, say "OK" as you lead her through.

❧ *Note: If the doorway is a big problem area, practice the preceding exercise five times in a row. By the fifth time, you should be making some progress.*

Using WAIT in the Car

Once you've mastered using the WAIT command in the house, try using it in the car. Most dogs get pretty excited about a ride. Jump in, jump out. Yahoo! And you're left holding onto the end of the leash for dear life. Another embarrassment. However, it can and should change. Aside from your personal humiliation, you're sending your dog the wrong message. Your permissiveness communicates approval. Now do you really approve? I doubt it. Here's what you're going to do:

Getting into the Car:
1. Take your dog to your car. Instruct "WAIT."
2. Open the door.
3. If he jumps, say "NO!" and snap him back.
4. Re-command "WAIT."
5. Snap back harder, if necessary.
6. Once he stops his shenanigans, say "OK," and in he goes.
7. When he's in the car, instruct "WAIT" as you shut the door, leaving his leash on for now.

Your job is half over. After waiting twenty seconds, try the following:

Getting out of the Car:
1. Instruct "WAIT" before you open the car door.
2. Open it just a crack. A centimeter. If your dog lunges, snap it shut and repeat "WAIT!"
3. Repeat this procedure until your dog stops lunging.
4. Once you're able to open the door, grab for the leash. (If you miss the leash, just put your dog in the car and start over. No big deal.)
5. Repeat "WAIT" as you brace him with a firm arm.
6. When he pauses, command "SIT," and release him with an "OK!"

If this exercise was challenging and you can repeat it a few times without having a heart attack, do.

Some dogs take the car thing a bit too far. Allowed to jump in and out at will, they think the car is just another area of their domain. These fellows can be quite bothersome. Jumping from seat to seat, barking like lunatics, or demonstrating the really bad body-slam-to-the-window aggression response. All of which get, you know, attention. If this sounds too familiar, check out my suggestions on car restraint and problem solving.

PUPPY OWNERS

If you'd like to help avoid problems getting your dog in and out of the car, start early. Take your pup to the car. Instruct "SIT," positioning her if necessary. Next, tell her "WAIT" as you open the door. If she's a little anxious, pull her back and hold her in place. Pause, then say "OK" as you lean forward and pat the seat. Once she's in, instruct "SIT" and scratch her head for a few moments. One more "WAIT" as you close the door and you're halfway there. Pause five seconds, and say "WAIT" before you open the door. Catch your pup's leash if she rushes forward, and re-command "WAIT" as you prop her into a sitting position on the seat. When she settles, say "OK!" as you let her exit the car.

At this point, your dog should perk up every time he hears you say "WAIT." Start using it when you're out visiting friends or when you bring him to the veterinarian, groomer or dog school. In these situations, your structure communicates leadership. Tell him "WAIT" at each threshold. Although he may protest initially, hold him behind you. When he calms down, say "OK" as you lead him in. It gets easier, I promise!

Using WAIT with Company

We'll be covering this situation throughout the book. For now, "WAIT" is an essential part of your dialogue. Once your dog is a master of its meaning in a one-on-one situation, use the command around company. Here are two options for the arrival scene:

1. Create a station in the greeting area. When someone visits, secure your dog and tell him "WAIT" as you answer the door.

2. Hold him back as you go to the door, and instruct "WAIT" as you open it.

3. As you open the door, ask your company to ignore your dog until he's settled down. No eye contact, please. If he's stationed, just ignore him until he's quieted down. If you're leading him, control his enthusiasm with leash corrections only and give him the same silent treatment. Once he's bordering on normalcy, let him know he's welcome. Good dog!

NO

NO is one of the most important commands your dog must learn. I know, it's obvious, but few know the true meaning of the word. Some dogs hear it so much they confuse it with their name. Before we begin, however, I want you to do the following experiment with a human friend:

1. Pick a person over twelve years old. (Let's assume you asked a girl to help you.)

2. Show her a pencil.

3. Ask her to take it and to write a sentence.

4. After she's started writing, say "NO, NO, NO" loudly above her head. (I know this sounds ridiculous. She won't have any idea what you're shouting about. The experiment is only half over. You can use the same person or pick someone else.)

5. Ask her to take the pencil from you.

6. As she lifts her arm to reach for the pencil, say "NO" before she takes hold of it.

Her hand should freeze. I know mine would. It's fascinating when you think about it. Interrupt a thought process, and you can stop any action in an instant, whether it's a human reaching for a pencil or a dog contemplating a sock.

NO is one of the most important
commands to teach your dog.

To teach your dog the NO command, you must also interrupt the thought process. Before we go into its conversational application, practice this exercise (with your dog on her Teaching Lead):

1. With your dog in the next room, place a plate of cookies on the floor.
2. Holding your dog on the Teaching Lead, approach the plate.
3. The very second your dog notices the plate, snap the lead back firmly and say "NO!"
4. Walk by the cookies.
5. If your dog shows any interest whatsoever, repeat the procedure.
6. Play this game tomorrow—with some cheese or steak, perhaps!

Pretty soon, your dog will see a plate on the floor and turn his nose toward the sky. *"I don't see anything!"* Now you're ready to start using the command around everyday distractions. Try it with one of your snacks. Keeping your dog on a leash, sit in a chair. Have an Oreo. A chip. A rice cake, perhaps. If his nose shifts in your direction, snap the leash back and say "NO!" Do this without making eye contact. No, you're not teasing him. He must learn that not all food is his. He'll be more pleasant at dinner time. Calmer during the kids' snack time. A welcome party guest. And a fine addition at neighborhood barbecues.

Once you've got the food thing clear, try using the NO command whenever he's too attentive to the countertops. If he's off-lead, stamp your foot as you say "NO!" Perfected that? Now it's time to hit the road. Whenever your dog alerts to a bike, a jogger, a friend from the neighborhood, or a car, give his leash a quick tug as you say "NO!" Immediately refocus his attention with "LET'S GO" and praise him.

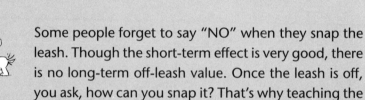

THE LEASH SNAP–"NO" CONNECTION

Some people forget to say "NO" when they snap the leash. Though the short-term effect is very good, there is no long-term off-leash value. Once the leash is off, you ask, how can you snap it? That's why teaching the term "NO" and pairing it with a leash snap is so important. Done together, they begin to mean the same thing. Your dog will eventually associate the word "NO" with the leash snap, so when the leash is off, a simple "NO" will do.

"What do I do once my dog has already snatched the chicken off the dinner table?"

Forget it. Yes, I'm serious. Once she's got the chicken, it's gone. Think back to the pencil example. Correcting a dog once she's in the act of eating makes about as much sense as shouting at your friend while she's writing a sentence. Neither animal's going to have any idea what you're driving at. A dog might wonder, "What are you mad about? My chewing? The way I slobber when I eat? My grunting sounds? What?" Or, upon closer examination, she might be interpreting your reaction as prize envy. She thinks that you think and act like a dog. When you approach her immediately after she's gotten hold of something new, your body tense and your tone threatening, she considers your actions not as discipline but as prize envy. I know it's hard, but let it go.

"Does the same attitude apply for stolen laundry?"

Yes. The same attitude applies.

"My puppy loves to grab everything on the ground. Is it safe?"

I wouldn't go so far as to say it's safe, but if you pay too much attention, you'll be reinforcing the activity. Obviously, you should observe what goes into your puppy's mouth, although if you make a big fuss each time he grabs for something, he might interpret your fast motions as prize envy and start swallowing his finds. Instead of making an issue out of your puppy's curiosity, try to refocus his attention on toys (plastic bottles are marvelous, and so are squeak toys tied to strings).

SETTLE DOWN

This command's a real beauty. So simple. So applicable. So conversational. I'll expand on the joys of its application momentarily. For now, you must go through the teaching process:

1. Pick a half-hour block of time. You can be watching TV, helping the kids with their homework, working on the computer, sewing, reading, etc.
2. Place your dog's lead on his buckle collar (not his training collar), and sit down.
3. Instruct "SETTLE DOWN," and point to the spot next to your left side.
4. Help him into a down position.

5. Quickly step on the leash. He should have only enough freedom to lie still.

6. Withdraw your attention for half an hour.

7. No, I'm not joking. Thirty minutes. No toys, attention, soothing, nothing.

8. At the end of thirty minutes, release him with "OK!"

9. Now, you can hug him.

Once your dog knows his station, he'll go automatically.

Initially, this exercise can be a real bear. Some dogs like to twist and shout. It's a control thing. Some dogs have a problem giving up control. They've got to relinquish it, however, if you're going to get anywhere training. After several days, he'll calm down, provided you don't give in.

I equate teaching the SETTLE DOWN command with teaching a child to sit still at the dinner table. It's all part of life. If kids don't learn manners, they end up with the initial ferocity of Helen Keller. (By the way, one of the best movies to watch if you're serious about dog training is *The Miracle Worker*. Are you siding with the parents or with her teacher? Three cheers for Annie Sullivan.) Kids have to learn to sit still, and so do dogs.

Once you've mastered using the command in controlled settings, try testing it in more stimulating situations—around family gatherings, or during mealtimes or company visits. When you're accomplished in these situations, try using it outside or when visiting friends or your veterinarian. Being able to use the SETTLE DOWN command is quite impressive. It's not only good for your ego, but it gives your dog a command to rely on. Everybody's relaxed.

"I'm not totally clear. Why must dogs learn to settle down?"

Good question. Several reasons. The first goes back to when the leader wolf would make one sound to send all the pack members running for cover. They trusted the sound. They never questioned it. It was a survival thing. They stayed put until he made another sound indicating that all was safe. Your sound is "SETTLE DOWN." Someday it may be a life or death thing; for now, it's about leadership. You want your dog to be still, and he must. Why? Because you said so.

In addition, this exercise teaches self-control. Dogs are born with it and use it naturally around mom, but many lose it when brought into their human homes. Humans tend to be too permissive with young pups. This exercise brings the self-control back. It helps check dominant dogs and notifies the more submissive types that someone is taking charge. What a relief.

"What if my dog won't go down?"

Some dogs totally resist the concept of being put into a submissive (down) position. If yours growls or snaps, do not proceed with this exercise; you need professional help to off-set present or potential aggression. On the other hand, if your dog is just stubborn, place the base of the leash under your foot and stand on it until your dog settles down. He'll look uncomfortable, I know. That's the motivation. When he lies down, release just enough slack to enable him to lie down comfortably, keeping your foot on the leash until the thirty minutes is up. 🐾 *Tip: During this procedure, your dog must have on his buckle collar.*

"Should I keep my foot on the leash the whole time?"

Initially, yes. If your dog gets up, you won't have to bat an eye. He'll look uncomfortable for a few minutes, then settle down again. After a couple of weeks, you'll notice his cooperation and you can loosen your controls. If he gets up too much, though, get that foot back on the lead!

"What about the STAY command?"

We'll get to it. I avoid using it here because I like a dog to know that when he hears "SETTLE DOWN," it means to stay until released.

OK, a situational puzzle!

Situation "SETTLE DOWN" #1

Emma, your Border Terrier, is going to see her veterinarian. For the past two weeks, you've been practicing the Magic Seven with great success, although you've never pushed your control beyond the house. When you get to the hospital, Emma's very excited, but she must wait her turn. Do you:

a) Pick her up?
b) Repeat "SIT" fifteen times, eventually positioning her?
c) Say "SETTLE DOWN" to Emma, tucking her into position and stepping on the leash, and sit quietly with a magazine until her name is called?

What'd you guess? (c)? Congratulations. Two weeks is a good foundation. Although picking her up would have been the easiest solution, she would have felt more threatened and defensive (resulting in yapping or nipping) when back on the ground. Whether you have a little dog or a big dog, you want to encourage good ground-level coping skills.

Those commands are your Magic Seven! Remember to use them conversationally throughout the day. Good luck!

UNIVERSAL DISCIPLINE

There is one Universal Discipline. One that works on every dog. Granted, it works to varying degrees, but it works. What is it? *The withdrawal of attention*. This is a concept I keep repeating over and over. Quite simply, there are times when you must ignore your dog.

I can already hear voices of protest. And I'd agree, you can't always turn the other cheek. We'll cover the more serious infractions in Chapter Seven. But there are many behaviors you can and should overlook. More than you'd imagine. Here are five examples.

The Passive Director

These guys thrive on attention, and when they're not getting it, they feel insecure. To alleviate their stress, they demand attention; however, if you respond, what are you reinforcing? That's right, their insecurity. You're also following their direction and disappearing from your leadership role, which leads to more insecurity. More stress. You don't want to do that. When your passive pooch is pawing, whining, head-butting, staring, barking or hiding under your legs, ignore him. Yes, ignore him. I know it may sound cruel, but if you coddle the insecure dog, you get an insecure dog. Stand tall, relax, and be a pillar of serenity, and he'll calm down. He'll start looking up to you. His leader. And when he does, reinforce that with—what else?—your love and attention!

The Active Director

These guys thrive on reminding you of their leadership. They try many of the same ploys as their passive counterparts, but they calculate their successes. It's a different approach—much more demanding. And if you pay attention to these characters, you're reinforcing their dominance. You don't want to do that either. So use the same tactic as for the passive director dogs: ignore them. They'll be more persistent and more annoying, but remember their motive, and be strong.

The Grab-n-Go

Dogs think this is a riot. . . . *I grab sock. Show the household. Wait in my usual play bow until someone notices! Then I fake left. Dart right. Dodge for the table. Under the legs. Up the stairs. And for the big finale. . . I'll hide under one of the beds.* The little comedian. It's quite addictive. Meanwhile, the entire household has been disrupted, and everyone is racing around like crazy, laughing at the entire scene. Take-home message: A great game!

Relating? Let me make a suggestion. When your dog starts baiting you, leave the room, the house or the yard. Shut all the doors behind you. Dogs hate this. Yours will wonder where you went and forget about the game. If she's got an object you can't ignore, however, avoid making eye contact with her initially. Wait a few minutes, then change her focus by shaking her biscuit box. When she comes to you, leash her and rescue the object later when she's not watching. Corrections, after all, are a form of attention. Remember the pencil.

The Noise Maker

These guys love the spotlight, and if they're not in it, you're going to hear about it. I've read a bizzillion techniques for remedying this situation and found that nothing works better than a patient dose of the silent treatment. Whether your dog is stationed or crated, if you give him attention, even negative attention, you're reinforcing his behavior. Now, wouldn't you rather have a quiet dog? Of course you would, so pay attention to that! ❧ *Tip: Buy yourself some wax ear plugs while you're doing the silent-treatment bit.*

The Runaway

I don't recommend off-lead activities for untrained dogs. Invariably, they'll wander off and master the fun of staying just out of reach. This is tremendously annoying and counterproductive to future off-lead work. The reality, however, is that your dog may get away from you before his off-lead training has begun. The kids may leave the door open, he could jump out of the car, or his leash could break. There are two options for these emergency situations:

- Run away from your dog quickly while calling out in order to get his attention. I've been known to bolt in the opposite direction, shrieking like a baboon to get a dog's attention. You can hop in the car, run inside, hide behind a tree, or whatever. Just disappear! Dogs find this fascinating. If he follows, praise him profusely, even if you're mad.

- If your dog really takes off, follow him quietly. Shouting is equated with barking and reinforces his excursion. When you finally get him, praise him. I know you're mad, but if you discipline him, he'll never trust your approaches.

HOW TO IGNORE A JUMPING DOG

It's difficult. You *can* correct him. You can also ignore him. Both methods work and are effective. Ignoring your dog, however, is a more passive and positive approach. To do it, fold your arms in front of you like a pouting child and raise them to your eye level. Stare at the ceiling. Dogs hate this. Once he's quit jumping, let your arms down, but continue to deny attention until he has completely settled down. This technique also works wonders when you're coming into the house from running errands or school. Encourage everyone to use the same approach, and the message will spread like fire.

"Let me get this straight. I should ignore my dog instead of correct him?"

Yes. For the minor attention-getting routines. I know, hitting a dog over the head with a saucepan is more tangible, but aside from the fact that it's cruel, it's still attention. As hard as it may be for you, give my "ignore him" suggestion a try for one week. Pretty soon, you'll be a believer, too.

"What should I do about unsuspecting visitors?"

Some visitors can help out, postmen and spouses' bosses not excluded. When someone arrives, place your dog on her Teaching Lead and either lead or station her by the door, as outlined in Chapter Two. Refocus her enthusiasm with a favorite toy, and correct any jumping with a snap of the lead and "SSHHH!" Ask your company to ignore her until she is calm. After she's settled down, bring her to the company, instruct "SIT," and praise calmer interactions.

THE POWER OF PRAISE

Who can argue? Praise just feels good. It feels good when we get it; it feels good to give it. It's the universal motivator—and I haven't even begun talking dogs yet!

Dogs are no different then we are. To see just how responsive they are to praise, I want you to try an experiment for one week. Just one week. Here it is:

1. Look at your dog when she is good. Only when she's good. If she's acting up, ignore or discipline her without making eye contact.
2. Encourage good behavior by using your Teaching Lead, as described in Chapter Two.
3. Praise your dog warmly whenever she's calm, resting or chewing a bone. Pet her, stare lovingly into her eyes, and tell her how glad you are to have her.
4. When your dog settles down at a station, pet and praise her, as I described before.

Give it one week. Magically (it will seem), you'll see the scales of behavior start to tip. She'll calm down, and so will you! Beautiful.

Here's the final situational puzzle of this chapter:

Situation "Praise Power" and "Universal Discipline"

Disney is a ten-month-old Lhasa Apso. A mop of blond hair, he's so cute he's almost edible. Loving the spotlight, if he's ignored, he puts on quite a show to bring it back. Pawing, barking, and dancing on two legs are all part of his repertoire. Lately, however, he's been running away from his adoring owners outside, and the neighbors are beginning to complain of his barking when he's left alone. To help remedy this situation, would you suggest:

a) They buy another dog to keep Disney company?

b) Discipline Disney firmly for running away and shout at him when he barks?

c) Ignore Disney's attention-getting tactics, pet him when he's calm, use a leash outside, and start a training program immediately?

Did you pick (c)? Yeah! Getting another dog would be a disaster at this point; Disney would teach him all his bad habits. Maybe later, when Disney's trained. As for choice (b), discipline would only reinforce the activity or frighten Disney. Not good. The perfect solution is (c). Disney will learn that his owners are in charge and practice the art of calmness!

Wow, this was a big chapter! Now it's on to heartier matters. With this foundation, though, you'll find advanced training a snap.

Chapter 4

Basics for Your Best Friend

Okay. I'm going to come right out and say it. Your dog doesn't know too much human stuff. Oh, she's intelligent all right, but she's just a dog. She doesn't sit around contemplating complex sentence structure and vocabulary. She'll know plenty as soon as you teach her, but for now it's not making a whole lot of sense. Take a look at this example:

OWNER: *"Daisy, come. Come on, please. Come. Come. Right now. I'm running late. Please come—I'll give you a biscuit. Biscuit. Biscuit. Come on, Daisy. Daisy. Ugh!"*

DAISY: *Doesn't she look ridiculous? I think she'd be happier over here rolling in this sweet scent with me. Why is she running at me? She looks scary. Uh-oh, I better run back, fake left and stay away.*

OWNER: *"Sit. Sit-sit-sit. Really, she's obedience-trained. Daisy, stay. Get down. Stay. Stop jumping on the nice man. Stay. Stay. Sit-sit-sit."*

DAISY: *A visitor. My favorite time of the day. I'm so excited. When I jump, everyone moves and pays attention. How fun! Jumping must be good.*

OWNER: *"Daisy, heel. Heel. Heel."* Arm wrestling and choking dear Daisy into position.

DAISY: *I don't understand what's taking my breath away. I feel like I'm being strangled. I want to get away. "Heel" must mean something bad.*

So, you see? Your dog may be the most intelligent one you know, but she can't understand how to respond until you teach her properly. The best methods for teaching provide a structured environment and positive reinforcement. Good teachers take their job seriously and know the learning process is gradual. They avoid frustration, hitting, isolation and yelling.

In this chapter, we'll cover the following commands:

HEEL

STAY

DOWN

COME

And in the "Game Gallery" section at the end of the chapter, I'll show you how you can use different games to practice mastering the commands.

These commands are the basics. Nothing fancy. No showy stuff. Adequate for your family dog, your best friend, your companion. I've listed the commands in the order we'll learn them. I know. The COME command is your highest priority, and it's listed last. Each command, however, relies on the command before it, so don't rush ahead. Breathe deeply. Lots of patience.

In the last chapter, we laid a foundation of understanding between you and your dog. You lead, she follows. You taught your pal seven commands. In this chapter, we'll be extending her vocabulary by using a similar approach. Conversational. Friendly.

Each new command has a three-stage process: 1) Tell and Show, 2) Ask and Appreciate, and 3) Request and Enforce. Don't worry. Breaking it down makes it easier. Here's a quick explanation:

Tell and Show: You'll give your dog the command "SIT" as you praise and position her.

Ask and Appreciate: Sooner or later, she'll start beating you to the punch line. Your praise encourages her cooperation.

Request and Enforce: After your dog recognizes a command, you'll enforce the response without physical guidance. At this stage, you can expect obedience in everyday situations.

Tell and show. *Beth Wright.*   Request and enforce. *Beth Wright.*

Practice all three stages of training on your Teaching Lead, which will give you a solid foundation for the off-lead exercises in the next chapter. How quickly you move from one stage to the other will depend on your dog. Some learn faster than others, just like people. I have always approached the initial stages of training slowly, even with my most brilliant dogs. Simple training steps makes them feel successful and good about working with you.

With each new command, you'll practice Stage One in lesson time only. Your lessons should last no more than two to three minutes and should end with lots of praise, a game or a walk. After you've practiced Stage One for a week or so, you'll begin to bring the command into everyday situations as described in Stage Two exercises. And as you work to bring one command out of lesson time (Stage Two), you'll start working another command into lesson time (Stage One). Confused? Cross-eyed? It will all make sense in a minute. Let's begin!

HEEL

This command is great. One of my favorites. Eventually, you'll be able to use it to walk your dog calmly around any distractions, to call your dog to your side, and to instruct your dog to lie at your side when you are entertaining houseguests. Honestly! It can happen. With the right training approach, you can make anything can happen.

Tell and Show

When introducing this command, pick an area free from distractions. Outside is fine as long as you avoid heavy distractions. Inside will do provided you can clear an area large enough to practice in. Eliminate as many distractions as possible.

Your first efforts will be to teach your dog to identify the HEEL command as a position next to you. Whether you're walking or standing, when you say "HEEL," your dog must stay at your side in the Directional Position.

This position looks like this:

The HEEL command, tell and show.
Diana Postell.

It's a pretty picture. It encourages focus. Your heels are ahead of your dog's paws. Your head and feet are aligned. If you're walking, your dog is walking; if you stop, you teach the dog to sit automatically. ❧ *Tip: How many ways were you taught to sit in a chair? No, it's not a trick question. How many? Who said "one"? You're right. One way. And who taught you? Right again. Your parents. Now guess how many ways there are to sit or walk at a heel? One. One way. And since you're the parent, you must teach that. Dogs, like kids, will test lots of ways. They'll sit backwards, behind you, or face you. Sometimes just to pull your pant leg. But like a good parent you'll enforce the one position.*

Once you pick your area, pattern a circle. Not a square, rectangle or triangle. A circle, nice and round. The diameter will depend on your dog. Small dog, smaller circle. Big dog, bigger circle.

Got the circle in your mind? Bring your dog to the edge, face in a counterclockwise direction (dog on the inside of the circle), and command "HEEL" as you position your dog in a sit at your side. Yes, I did say "HEEL," not "SIT." You must teach your dog to equate the HEEL command with a position next to yoxether stationary or walking.

Before you begin walking, check yourself. Are you relaxed? Standing tall? Looking confident with the lead around your waist? OK, then. Adjust the training collar either between your dog's ears (for the chain or self-correcting collar) or under the dog's chin (for the chin lead). The collar should be relaxed, though no slack should remain in the lead. To keep your dog walking in the proper position, bring your left arm behind your back as if you were going to stick your thumb in a back pocket. This is your starting position. Deep breath!

Now you can begin:
1. Say "HEEL" as you step forward.
2. Walking at an upbeat pace, keep your left arm behind your back.
3. Use wrist checks to keep her attention. Praise all focus.
4. Initially, stop after each circle.
5. Before you stop, slow your pace to get your dog's attention.
6. Keep your arm back, and stop abruptly, clicking your heel for added emphasis.
7. Remind "HEEL" as you position your dog into a sit at your side.

8. If you're having trouble getting your dog to sit when you stop, grasp the lead with your right arm extended along your left leg, pull upwards, and position her with your left hand as you say "HEEL."

For the first few days, practice six circles. This should take no more than three minutes. Keep your pace steady even if your dog stops dead or races forward. You're the leader, the pacemaker. You create the rhythm.

After a few days, you can start adding pace changes and turns to your normal routine:

Fast Pace: Start normally, then increase your speed. Cluck to encourage your dog's focus. Trot like a horse to encourage interest. Before you stop, slow into a normal pace.

Slow Pace: Start normally, then slow your pace. Like a snail. A tortoise. Lengthen your stride to encourage your dog's focus.

Turns: Start normally, then remind "HEEL" as you pivot away from your dog. Not a U-turn, just a linear pivot. Slap your left leg and bend your knees to encourage your dog's focus. Walk in the opposite direction, then stop.

Keep these practice sessions short, up-beat and consistent. End each one with a ton of praise and a favorite game!

In Summary:
1. Pattern a circle, and keep your dog on the inside.
2. Using the command "HEEL," place your dog in the Directional Position, stand tall, and hold the leash behind your back.
3. Start with "HEEL" and walk at a steady pace.
4. If your dog drags or bolts, do not change your rhythm; steady yourself, and use wrist snaps to encourage participation.
5. To stop, tap your heel as you bring your right hand across your body to pull the leash up. If necessary, use your left hand to position the dog in a sit.

Reading this on paper actually makes it sound easier than it is. Initial problems are the rule rather than the exception. Don't feel bad. I once tripped in the middle of a four-way intersection. Quite embarrassing. If you're having trouble, go though this checklist:

1. Are you standing tall? Bent body posture encourages play.
2. How's that tone? It must be directional, not playful or angry.
3. Stop watching the dog! When you're heeling, look in front of you.
4. Avoid physical contact until the lesson is over. Some dogs get too stimulated when touched. Praise warmly without petting.
5. Get a straight sit. If your dog's crooked, chances are she's focused on something else. And if that's so, your lesson is doomed. Encourage focus from the start by insisting on that directional position.

"Do dogs get confused when HEEL is used for SIT?"

I honestly don't know. I imagine it's confusing in the beginning, but then again so was algebra. They pick it up quickly though. I've found that in the long run it makes more sense to teach the HEEL command as a position. Your dog walks if you're walking, sits if you're still. If your dog is totally clueless, you can say "HEEL-SIT-HEEL" as you stop in the beginning. Then wean off "SIT" in a week.

"My dog refuses to sit straight. What should I do?"

First, you must determine whether you have a role to play. Are you giving your dog too much slack or holding your hand in front of your thigh? Are you standing crookedly? If you are, then you must consider your dog. She'll fall into one of two categories:

1. *The Confronter:* This dog turns to face you. She's more interested in play or resistance than in your leadership.
2. *The Daydreamer:* This one's likely to sit on your heels instead of in front of them. She's interested in everything *but* you!

If you've got a confronter, don't get offended. Get him into the Directional Position before making eye contact or praising. You can try two approaches: 1) Use your hands to scooch him into position. If that turns into a game . . .

WRIST CHECK

The wrist check is a preventative measure to use before your dog starts pulling. It jingles the chain and lets the dog know you're there. To check your wrist, just snap it front to back sternly. The chain should make a zipping sound. After each snap, remind "HEEL" and continue moving.

2) Grasp the base of the lead, step back on your left foot, and rotate him into position. Step forward as you bring his head into position behind you. When he's adjusted, look at him and praise him.

If you've got a daydreamer, don't take it personally. It's common. When she sits crookedly, side-step to the right and snap the lead to your left hip. If she should topple over, help her into position and praise her once she gets there.

"When I work in the grass, my dog gets very distracted."

Try pavement. Save grass work for the second stage of training.

"I think I have the most pain-insensitive dog in the world. None of the collars make much of an impression."

Try holding the lead behind your back. Grip the lead with both hands behind you, against your left hip. Take up enough slack to permit your dog to walk comfortably in the correct position. If she pulls, push back with your left hip.

"My dog refuses to heel. Every time we start out, he begins to paw and jump. It's like we're in battle!"

Could you be holding his lead too tightly, causing him to choke? If so, loosen the lead or try a chin lead. If not, then you've got a strong-willed boy on our hands—a real fighter. I know it's tempting to throw in the towel, but you can't lose this battle. If you do, you're trashing all your off-lead dreams, and I can't let you do that! Here's the solution:

- Don't fight back.
- Don't soothe your dog, and get rid of any guilty feelings you may have.
- Remember that you reinforce what you pay attention to.
- If you're concerned about choking your dog, buy a chin lead.
- The next time your dog kicks, keep going. Slowly, steadily, calmly.
- Do not make eye contact until he's walking well.
- Praise all focus and cooperation.

Ask and Appreciate

Your dog should have a good feeling when she hears "HEEL." Now's the time to begin using it in everyday situations and to teach her to come from a distance. You will work at this stage for a week or two, depending on your dog's cooperation!

The HEEL command, ask and appreciate. *Diana Postell.*

Here are some conversational applications:
- Practice during your walk.
- Practice some patterns indoors as you move from room to room.
- Give the command as you walk to the car.

Increase your control around distractions slowly. No living-room-on-Monday-and-freeway-on-Tuesday attempts, please!

The Return: This is really handy. Your goal is to call your dog into the Directional Position regardless of her distance from you or surrounding distractions. The first step, however, is to communicate your expectations. With your dog on a lead, practice this exercise four times throughout the day:

1. Let your dog walk out the extent of the lead.
2. Standing directly behind her tail, call out her name.
3. If she doesn't look, snap her chain. Praise her for focusing.
4. Next, command "HEEL" as you slap your left side.
5. Step backward as she comes to you, and praise.
6. Step forward as you rotate her into the Directional Position.
7. Encourage a straight sit and eye contact. Release with lots of praise! Good job!
8. Let her return to normal activities immediately. You don't want her to think the command is a life sentence!

The Rotate: There are two ways to rotate your dog into the Directional Position: around your right side or to the left. Which one you pick will depend on your dog. Try both to see what works best.

To rotate around to the right, take the lead in your right hand as your dog approaches. Stepping back, transfer the lead (and the dog) around your back side to your left hand. Draw your dog up against your left side, and finish by asking her to sit. To rotate around to the left, hold the lead in your left hand as your dog approaches. Take a giant step back on your left foot as you direct your dog into position. Step forward, ask her to sit, and praise!

The Leg Slap: Dogs are very sensory-oriented. They love sound and motion. The leg slap adds a little zing to the call back. As you say "HEEL," slap your left side and keep on slapping until she's in position. Eventually, one small slap will bring her into place!

THE ENFORCE

At this stage, you can begin to enforce your commands by using a corrective "NO" when your dog chooses not to listen. If she looks at a passerby, say "NO!" If she keeps sniffing when you call her, say "NO!" If you instruct "HEEL" when there is a guest in the house, but she decides not to listen, say "NO!" Issue a leash snap simultaneously to emphasize the negative.

You can also practice this exercise inside! Say "HEEL" before offering dinner, pats or treats. Help her rotate into position, and reward her enthusiastically!

One more great application. Try it when you're sitting in a chair. Command "HEEL" as you slap the side of your leg. Help your dog rotate into position, command "DOWN," and pet her lovingly. Eventually, you'll be able to call your dog with a slap and have her settle down when company is visiting. Quite an accomplishment!!!

Request and Enforce

You've been a patient teacher. You've put in your time. Now it's time to reap the benefits. Begin to use the HEEL command in normal everyday situations. Here are some examples:

- When you are walking in town, "HEEL" reminds your dog to stay focused on you.
- When the postman arrives, "HEEL" tells your dog to stop barking and check in with you. Eventually, she'll do it automatically—the perfect watchdog!
- On your walk, "HEEL" controls her as joggers, cars and other animals pass by.
- In the evening, "HEEL" calls her to your side for a pat.
- At dinner or other social events, "HEEL" settles her while you entertain.

Add to the list. The applications are endless!

The HEEL command, request and
enforce. *Diana Postell.*

Once you've mastered the preceding exercises on your Teaching Lead, practice calling your dog back to your side on the Flexi. Initially, call her back to your side from ten feet, then fifteen feet, then twenty-six feet (if yours extends that far). Cheer her on as she comes towards you. As she approaches, grasp the base of the Flexi to rotate her into the Directional Position.

"I've taught this command for a solid month. Sometimes, my dog still ignores me."

Patience, dear reader. She's testing to see whether you mean what you say. Like kids, dogs want to know whether we're paying attention to them. If your dog ignores you, check the leash, say "NO" and reel her in. Enforce your expectation every time. Soon she'll trust that when you say it, you mean it.

"Off-lead, my dog totally ignores me! It's so frustrating!!!"

Who said anything about off-lead? This chapter is about conditioning on-lead control. Now, about the frustration. We've all felt it. Yes, even me. However, don't let your dog know. Dogs don't understand frustration. They view tense body postures in one of two ways:

1. The active personalities see the tension as a play posture. The old catch-me-if-you-can!
2. The quiet personalities are confused. They get frightened and won't come near you.

In either scenario, getting frustrated doesn't exalt your leadership or bring your dog back to you. If your dog should slip away, walk into the house or get into the car (most dogs get curious and will follow), or stand calmly until your dog returns. For now, the best bet is to keep your dog leashed!

"When I'm sitting and call my dog, he has a hard time rotating into position."

Most do. Help him into position with your hands, denying eye contact and physical rewards until he's in place.

STAY

A lot of people fantasize about the STAY command. "My dog never sits still." Actually, it's not hard to teach if you take it slowly. Eventually, you'll be able to use it to steady your dog around distractions; calm your dog during greetings; settle your dog during mealtimes; and enforce a still position at a distance, such as across a street.

Yes, it can happen. Fairy tales can come true. But you must take it slowly! By approaching this command in stages, you'll build a positive success rate and enhance your dog's trust in this command. Trusting dog, confident owner. A beautiful equation. Are you ready? Let's begin!

Tell and Show

When teaching this command, select an area free from distractions. Indoors is best. Bring your dog to the area with the lead folded neatly in your left hand. Slide any neck collars between her ears. Since your dog is most familiar with the SIT command, we'll start with that one. Eventually, you will be able to get your dog to stay in any position.

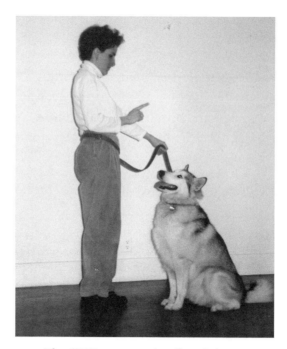

The STAY command, tell and show.
Sally Sarsfield.

Your Ready Position:
1. Command "SIT" at your left side.
2. Check your feet! Keep your heels in front of her paws.

3. Hold the lead above your dog's head at about hip level.
4. Command "STAY."

The **Easy Eight Exercises** for your eventual expert are these:

1. Pivot *six inches*—I repeat, six inches—in front of your dog.
2. Pause *five seconds*, return (feet ahead of paws), and release with "OK!"
3. Pivot six inches, pause *ten seconds*, return, and release.
4. Pivot, pause, and then *march*—yes, march—in place. Don't look into your dog's eyes.
5. Pivot, pause, and then start *walking side to side* very slowly. Stop back in front of your dog, return to her side, and release!
6. Pivot, pause, and then *make funny sounds*. Barnyard noises will do: moo, neigh, meow, quack! Just for a second, then return, and release with an "OK!" *Remember: no eye contact!*
7. Pivot and pause for *fifteen* seconds. Return, pause, praise and release.
8. Go for the *big hug*. Job well-done!

Who's wondering about steps three, four and five? Let me explain. Your goal is a solid stay regardless of distractions—marching bands and cattle herds not excluded. To reach this goal, however, you must start small. And the best way to do this is to be distracting yourself.

Once you've got the six-inch stay down to a science, try the following:

1. Intensify your distractions. Hop around, twist and shout, sound off like a wild orangutan; let your imagination run wild!
2. Increase your distance incrementally. One foot at a time. At each distance, introduce the distractions slowly.

Practice these exercises twice a day for a few minutes.

"Can you repeat the STAY command?"

Yes. Whenever introducing a new distraction or if your dog's about to break. Avoid run-on STAY commands, however: "STAY-STAY-STAY-DAISY STAY!" Give just one quick, stern reminder.

USING HAND SIGNALS

Signaling encourages visual focus, which is paramount in off-lead control. Give each signal with your right index finger as you're speaking your verbal commands.

"SIT": Sweep upwards from your dog's nose to your eyes with your index finger.

"STAY": Quickly flash your index finger in front of your dog's nose.

"OK": Sweep your index finger straight out from your dog's nose, adding lots of energy and praise for a job well-done!

"My dog does the stay part really well. She breaks when I return."

Make sure you keep your feet in front of her paws as you return. In addition, hold the lead above her head and remind "STAY" as you pivot back. If she breaks, check up and re-command "STAY" in a serious tone.

"How do you discipline movement?"

You don't discipline anything in the introduction stage. When practicing, hold the lead above your dog's head. If she thinks about breaking, pull it up and remind "STAY!" If she should get away from you, return her to the original starting point calmly and remind "STAY."

"What if my dog lies down?"

Go to her calmly, cup your fingers under her buckle collar, and lift her back into position (big dog owners, bend those knees!). Avoid using the chain to haul your dog up.

"Help! My dog keeps jumping on me!"

Quite a comedian. First of all, stop looking at her and don't laugh! Also avoid pushing her away, as pushing is considered confrontational play. Use the lead to snap her down off your body and back into position. Gaze calmly above her head and relax. Staring, shoving and a tense body postures make dogs jumpy.

"My dog growls. What should I do?"

You need professional help. You've got a budding aggressor on your hands.

"How do I know when to move onto the next stage?"

When you can act like a goon and sound like a monkey, with six feet between you and your dog, you're ready to move on.

Ask and Appreciate

Once you've made it to six feet, start using the SIT-STAY command around low-key distractions. Some examples are needed. Hmmm. Use a SIT-STAY when you do the following:
- sort laundry
- make the bed
- tie your kid's shoe

Add to the list! Be creative, and remember to command firmly and use those hand signals!

In addition, you can practice some fun exercises to reinforce your dog's understanding. Here are some of my favorites:

THE TUG TRIAL Instruct "STAY," and pivot two feet in front of your dog. Remind "STAY" as you tug gently on the lead. If your dog leans forward,

The SIT-STAY command, ask and appreciate.
Sally Sarsfield.

step toward her as you signal "STAY." As she improves her resistance, increase the intensity and distance—within reason.

SITUATIONAL SET-UPS   Set up everyday situations to practice your control. For example, if your dog gets bent out of shape when she hears the doorbell, you can rig that situation. Ask a friend to ring your doorbell. Tell your dog "SHHH!" to calm her excitement before you command "SIT-STAY." Ask your helper to ring the bell five times at twenty-second intervals; then have them disappear and come in another entrance. This deconditions your dog's thinking so that she does not associate every ring of a doorbell with the arrival of company. You can set up any situation! A person coming over to greet you, kids running by, cars going by, food temptations, the dishwasher being loaded. You name it!

THE DISAPPEARING ACT   Position your dog three feet from a corner. Command "STAY," and pivot to face him. Remind "STAY" as you disappear behind the corner for five seconds. Upon your return, avoid direct eye contact and remind "STAY." As you continue practicing, increase your duration and distance. This exercise enhances your dog's focus, even if you're not there to watch!

"I tried using STAY the other day when I dropped some nails. It didn't work too well."

Good for trying. "A" for effort. Now, set up the same situation. With your dog on her Teaching Lead, drop some nails, command "SIT-STAY," and be more attentive to corrections if they're needed.

"I tried that doorbell thing, and my dog went nuts!"

It sounds like the doorbell was too much. Try with a lower-level distraction. Opening and shutting the door, perhaps.

"My dog pops up the minute I disappear."

Don't worry. Hide yourself one body part at a time. A leg, a leg and an arm, a leg, an arm and a shoulder, etc.

"How do I know I'm ready for Stage Three?"

It's an inner feeling. You'll just know. Your dog will cooperate willingly, looking at you with eyes that say "I know that."

Request and Enforce

Continue working on the Teaching Lead. Off-lead applications are discussed in Chapter 5. Begin incorporating the STAY command into normal activities. Here are some handy applications for everyday use:
* When you're meeting a friend or helping someone with directions.
* When you're putting the kids on the bus: "No you can't go with them!"
* As you're signing for a package.
* To calm her before tossing a ball.

Add to the list!

The STAY command, request and enforce. *Sally Sansfield.*

Most dogs break their commands when they're initially exposed to intense distractions. I know, you've been working so hard. Your dog should reward you with complete attention. The key for you is to stay calm when your dog is overstimulated. Don't get bent out of shape. Your reaction must depend on your dog's mind-set. Yes, his mind-set. Is he breaking as a reaction to confusion or anxiety? Defiance or distractiveness?

If it's confusion or anxiety, don't correct him. It would only intensify his concern. Quietly take him back to his original spot, and remind "STAY." If he keeps breaking, he's telling you that you're asking too much. Slow down, as pressure kills cooperation.

If it's defiance or distractiveness, however, that's quite another story. You can't ignore defiance or distractiveness. To correct your dog, do the following:

1. Look to the ground as you go to your dog calmly.
2. Pick up the lead.
3. Snap it sternly as you say "NO."
4. Return him to the original spot.

5. Position firmly. Do not re-command "SIT."
6. Re-command "STAY," without eye contact.
7. Go back to whatever you were doing, giving your dog verbal assurance when he's calm.

If your dog keeps breaking, the situation may be too much to handle. Try an easier setting.

"What's the difference between WAIT and STAY?"

Great question. WAIT is an impulsive, spur-of-the-moment command—meaning "freeze!" You would use it, for example, to stop your dog momentarily when a car passes. The STAY command is more formal. It begins as a stationary command, like SIT, and ends in a formal release. You would use STAY on your dog if you stopped to help somebody in a car asking for directions.

"My dog scootches when we're around heavy distractions."

Ahhh. The old scootch routine. Smart dog. She's trying so hard. Give a quick tug of the leash, and tell her "SHHH." If she absolutely can't sit still, she's sending you a message that you're asking her for too much.

"My dog dashes from me when I go to reposition him."

Is your dog off-lead? If so, there's your problem. We'll get into the off-lead stuff next chapter. If he's on-lead, then perhaps you're approaching him threateningly or saying "NO" before you reach him. This reaction would concern any dog. Otherwise, you must determine whether your dog's anxious, in which case you'd reposition calmly, or defiant, in which case you'd:

1. Hang your head low as you calmly walk towards him.
2. Gently grasp the lead or collar.
3. Say "NO" as you return him to his original spot.
4. Remind "STAY."

"My dog mouths my hand as I reposition him."

He's protesting. Make sure you're not choking him. Otherwise, carry on and ignore the protest. Yes, ignore the protest. Attending to it would be perceived as interactive or confrontational. If he doesn't stop, hire a professional.

"When I go to reposition my dog, she cowers, though I've never mistreated her. What's that about?"

I don't know. Did you rescue your dog? There may be some history there. Could you be hovering over an already-passive dog? Try kneeling as you reposition. You'll look less threatening. Could you be correcting prematurely or marching over in an angry fashion? I'd cower, too. Ease off. Position calmly.

DOWN

Once you can get your dog to accept the DOWN command, you can ask for anything. Why? Because the down position communicates submission and vulnerability. A dog will do it if he trusts you. And when a dog trusts you, you can ask for anything.

Teaching this command, however, is not so poetic. Most dogs resist initially. Younger, more passive dogs are the most willing, but if you've got an ol' brut, brace yourself. You may be in for a struggle that you just can't lose! Now that I've prepared you for the worst, let's begin.

Tell and Show

There are three approaches to introducing this command. Selecting one will depend on, you guessed it, your dog.

The Easy Slide
This one is great for easy-going dogs or pups.
1. Instruct "SIT," and kneel down perpendicular to your dog's side.
2. Quickly draw a line from your dog's nose to the floor as you say "DOWN."

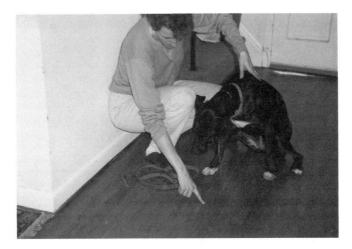

The DOWN command, tell and show. *Dona Flam.*

3. Place your left thumb in between her shoulder blades and . . .
4. Cup a front paw near the elbow with your right hand.
5. Gently lift the paw forward, as you firmly press between the shoulder blades—I repeat, the shoulder blades, not the neck.
6. Don't pet your dog yet! Pause five seconds, praising quietly verbally.
7. Release, stand up, and praise!

The Side Swipe

If your dog protests the Easy Slide method, try this one.

1. Sit your dog, and kneel at her side.
2. Point from her nose to the floor as you command "DOWN."
3. Place both hands on their corresponding paws, above the elbow.
4. Lay your left forearm across her shoulder blades.
5. Gently lift her legs as you apply pressure with your arm.
6. Re-command "DOWN" as you're positioning.
7. Pause five seconds, while praising verbally. Release with "OK," stand, and praise.

Look No Hands!

Has your dog confused her identity with that of Jaws? If so, try this method.

1. Command "SIT," and stand perpendicular to your dog's right side.

2. Holding the end of the lead, drop the slack on the floor and calmly slide it under your left foot. Fold the remaining slack in your left hand.

3. Command "DOWN" as you point to the floor.

4. Pull up on the lead continually, forcing your dog's head down.

5. Most dogs give in at this point. If yours does, praise verbally, pause, and release with "OK!"

6. If your dog doesn't respond, press her shoulder blades until she collapses into position, hold the slack under your foot for five seconds, and then release and praise.

🐾 *Note: If your dog's protesting aggressively (growls, snaps, has hard eyes—the works), call a professional. Immediately.*

Whatever method you choose, practice two to three times daily, four downs per session. Once your dog begins cooperating, use it in the following situations as well:

• Before treats: Holding the treat to the ground at her feet, say "DOWN."
• Before dinner: Covering the dish with a hand, place it on the ground and say "DOWN."
• Before a toy toss: Hiding the toy in your hand, hold the toy to the ground and say "DOWN."

🐾 *Note: Your dog may need a shoulder press to remind him. Release each object immediately!*

"My dog growls when I'm positioning him."

Go to the phone immediately, and get help from a professional dog trainer or behaviorist. You have a dominant dog who may bite when confronted with your requests.

"How can I stop the mouthing? My corrections seem to make it worse."

First of all, don't correct! It turns the command into a challenge game. Your dog's anxious. Let her know there's nothing to fear by ignoring her. Yes, ignore her. Allow your hand to go limp, stare at the wall in front of you, and ignore the situation until she settles. This communicates security and leadership.

If the mouthing really hurts, take your hand away slowly and try the 'No Hands' method.

"My dog rolls over when I give the command. How can I get him to stop his clowning?"

Whatever you do, don't pet his belly. This communicates approval. Stare at the wall, and ignore the situation until he's upright. Then praise him quietly. Release only when he's in the proper position.

"My dog goes right down, but he's back up again as quickly. What do I do?"

As soon as he's down, hold your hand to his shoulder blades and slide the lead under your foot so that he can't move. Release after he stops struggling.

"Can you command "DOWN" more than once?"

No. The DOWN command is like the SIT command. If you keep repeating it, it becomes a different sound. Repetition blurs clarity and lowers your dog's respect for your direction.

"How do you know when to go onto the next stage?"

When you, dog starts responding without your help. That might be four days or four weeks. Your dog will let you know.

Ask and Appreciate

You'll practice two exercises at this point: Distance Control and Situational Downs.

The DOWN command, ask and appreciate. *Dona Flam.*

Distance Control

Eventually, whether you're hanging upside down in a tree or shouting from across a football field, your dog will respond to this command. One step at a time, however. For now, practice:

1. Sit your dog, pivot perpendicularly, and casually slide the lead under your left foot.
2. Stand straight, and point to the ground as you command "DOWN" sternly.

3. Don't bend! Pull the lead under your foot continually.
4. Praise cooperation, pause, and release with an "OK."
5. If your dog refuses, press her shoulder blades.

Once your dog's responding, pivot six inches in front of her and . . .

6. Indiscreetly slide the lead under foot.
7. Lift your arm above your head. Point swiftly to the ground as you command "DOWN."
8. Pull the lead gently, if necessary. Press her shoulders if she refuses.
9. Pause, praise and release.

Once your dog's responding well at six inches, pivot out one foot and repeat the preceding steps. Then pivot from two feet, four feet, six feet, etc. You're on your way!

Situational Downs

Bring the DOWN command into nondistracting everyday situations, such as before you sit down to pet your dog, at night while you're watching TV or reading, or when your dog comes over for her good night kiss. Add to the list!

Remember the ration: one command, one action. If your dog responds, praise her lovingly. If she doesn't, position her calmly. Avoid getting frustrated as it only adds fear to an already stressful situation.

"Should we practice DOWN-STAYs?"

Once your dog goes down willingly, you can practice DOWN-STAYs. Do your drills in the same fashion as you do your SIT-STAYs.

"My dog scootches forward when I command DOWN from a distance. Should I discipline her?"

Not yet. Scootching is a sign of separation anxiety. Corrections only intensify it. Return to a distance she's comfortable with, and work back slowly. If the scootching continues, however, you may try the following:

1. Just before you give the command, lean forward and re-command "STAY."
2. Quickly command "DOWN" with a big hand signal.
3. If your dog responds, stand straight, pause, and return to release.
4. Position your dog in the original spot, if necessary.

Request and Enforce

Once your dog understands your expectations, use the DOWN command to ground her whenever a situation becomes chaotic or to settle her whenever you feel it's appropriate. Here are a few situations that come to mind:

- When company's visiting.
- At the veterinarian's office.
- When there's a sudden change in the environment.
- Outdoors, when she gets over-stimulated. Start small (squirrels), and work up to big (deer). Add to the list!

Remember to command once! Say "NO" if your dog ignores you as you position firmly.

"Why do you start using discipline at this stage?"

Great question. By this time, your dog has a positive association to the command. Since she understands what you're asking, "NO" corrects her for ignoring you. She must learn to filter your directions out from all other distractions.

"We learned the SETTLE DOWN command in Chapter 3. What's the difference between SETTLE DOWN and DOWN?"

You use the DOWN command when you're requesting an immediate response. SETTLE DOWN, you use to tell your dog to move to a specific spot and to stay until released.

"My dog scootches around on her belly when there's something stimulating. How do I correct her?"

You try not to. Ignoring often helps. Stepping on the lead can do the trick. If all else fails, wait until she's out of place, act astonished, and reposition her sternly with "SHHH!"

"My dog doesn't listen when other dogs are around. What should I do?"

Join a class. It's a lot of fun, great socialization and very helpful if you have the right teacher. Ask around your neighborhood and/or call your veterinarian. If you have some choices, view ongoing classes before you select.

"My dog is very fearful at the veterinarian's office. Should I force her down?"

You can use a TOWN DOWN once you've practiced it at home. I love this application. Here's how it goes:

1. Place a chair in the middle of a room.
2. Fold the lead up neatly in your left hand.
3. As you sit down, point under the chair and command "DOWN."
4. Grasp the leash under your knees, and thread her into position.
5. Slide the leash under your foot, and command "STAY."

You've done your first TOWN DOWN! So-called because it works great when you're out on the town. Once you've mastered this command at home, try it on the park bench, at a barbecue, when visiting a neighbor, or in your veterinarian's waiting room!

COME

At long last, the command you've been waiting for. A quick poll before we begin. . . .

How many of you, after calling once, have ever:
- Repeated yourself?
- Chased your dog?
- Brought out the cookies?
- Followed and captured your dog and then gotten angry?

Well, I hate to tell you, but you are teaching your dog the opposite of "COME." Your intentions may be good, but you're reinforcing disobedience. Quite a problem. Let's take a closer look.

Imagine someone asking you to leave something you're enjoying. Imagine that. You're sitting across the room, engrossed in a TV show or an article or tasting an incredible pastry, and suddenly someone calls you. "COME!" Your first impulse? My guess it'd be to filter out the request and stay focused on your own interest.

For dogs, "COME" is no less of a concept. Their immediate, untrained impulse will not be to drop everything and run joyfully to you. The response to the COME command is not that instinctive, trust me. On the other hand, it is possible to teach them the proper response by using a lot of structure, enthusiasm, patience, and praise. If you're ready and willing, let's begin!

Tell and Show

Like HEEL, the COME command is taught as a specific position. It tells your dog to take her place in front of you, whether you're calling from across the room or the yard. Your dog should sit directly in front of you and look into your eyes. Paws facing toes. Eye to eye. Good dog!

There are a few rules for teaching this command:

1. *Use it sparingly.* When it's over-used, dogs stop paying attention.
2. *Don't chase your dog if she doesn't respond!* Practice on-lead for now. We'll discuss off-lead applications in the next chapter.
3. *Surround the COME command with positives.* Use it in lessons and whenever you're offering something good, like attention, food or toys.
4. *Never call for negatives:* If you must retrieve your dog for grooming, isolation, or discipline, find her and escort her calmly. Don't use the COME command or get frustrated; this only creates fear.

WHAT DOES IT MEAN?

Has your dog gotten a backwards message? Does she think "COME" means to run away from you? If so, you're not alone. The real trouble is not the behavior itself, but your response to it. Bribing your naughty dog with treats, or heralding the command fifty times, or chasing her as she explores the neighborhood is what's really getting you into trouble. You're communicating that "COME" is the start of one big game. Fortunately, you can right the confusion, although it will take some time and concentration from the both of you. Don't worry too much, though. I've made the steps easy to follow and the training motivational!

5. *If your dog runs away, don't correct her!* I know the frustration of marching around in the middle of a cold, wet night calling your dog, but corrections only deteriorate trust. And trust is the first ingredient in a reliable response to the COME command.

6. *Use a different command to bring your dog inside.* Coming in from outdoors is a big drag, right up there with being left alone or ignored. Using the COME command to call your dog inside would make your dog associate it with a negative experience. Instead, pick a command like INSIDE. Start using it on-lead when bringing your dog into the house. Quickly offer a treat or ball toss.

Here are two introductory exercises: the Face Front and Traditional Taps.

Face Front

This fun exercise encourages enthusiasm and understanding. Practice it throughout the day. Here's how it goes:

1. Walk in front of your dog while she's standing calmly.
2. Say "DAISY, COME" as you stamp your foot and signal from her nose to your eyes. Make funny sounds to encourage a straight sit and focus.

3. If she doesn't respond, position the sit and wait until she has focused her eyes on yours before petting her.

4. Once she's positioned, give her a big hug!

Repeat this exercise throughout the day, whether you're offering a treat or a toy, to ensure that your dog's first association with the COME command will be rewarding and fun!

Traditional Taps

Practice this exercise in a quiet room. Turn off the TV, quiet the children, and close the blinds. Let nothing distract from the lesson at hand! Keep your lesson short and upbeat, as usual. Follow these steps:

1. Practice three SIT-STAYs, regular SIT-STAYs. Return to your dog's side, and release her with "OK!"

2. Leave your dog in a STAY, and walk out to the end of the leash.

3. Pause. Vary the duration each time.

4. Call "DAISY, COME!" in a directional tone.

5. As soon as you've issued the command, scurry backward and reel in the leash.

6. When she gets near your feet, tap your heel to the floor as you help her rotate into the proper sitting position.

7. Encourage eye contact by standing tall and making kissing sounds.

8. Release her with "OK!"

The COME command, tell and show. *Andrea Saas.*

Practice this exercise three times per session. That's all. More is stressful. ALSO! Do a few regular SIT-STAYs between each COME. If you don't, your dog will break her STAY early to please you. Sweet thing.

Pretty soon, your dog will run to you, sit automatically, and look up for approval. No magic, just good old-fashioned conditioning. You've reached the goal. Congratulations.

"How much time will it take for my dog to learn COME?"

I wish I could tell you. Every dog is different. Some get it in a few days; others, in a few weeks. Be patient and positive. You want your dog to love this command.

"What's the difference between the COME and HEEL commands?"

A specific spot. The HEEL is a position next to you. The COME is a position—a specific spot—in front of you, facing up. HEEL allows mutual attention to a situation, like someone coming to the door. COME communicates exclusive focus on your control; good for when the neighbor passes with a dog. COME, as you've probably guessed, is harder. It takes more concentration.

"My dog sits crookedly when she reaches me."

Straighten her out! To encourage a straight sit, slide the training collar underneath the chin, stand straight, and use a low tone of voice.

"My dog comes when I call him, but he's so excited that he jumps all over me!"

Your dog reminds me of one of my students. Jack is a big, blocky black Labrador Retriever whose enthusiasm might knock you flat. When his owner calls him, we all duck for cover, other dogs included. It's a positive problem, though, so don't get me wrong. To tone down a reaction such as this, do the following:

1. Command in a calmer voice.
2. As your dog comes, lean forward, with your arms outstretched like a flagger. (This blocking posture slows the dog down. Stand as he approaches.)
3. Say "SHHH" as he gets closer.
4. Stand tall and click your heels to finish.

"My dog stops three feet in front and veers to one side, licks my face, or tinkles."

You're probably bending over. You're in her way. Try leaning back when you call. Bent postures communicate play, confrontation or submission. Straight posture communicates confidence.

"My dog comes too fast for me to reel in the lead."

Another positive problem with an easy solution. As soon as you've said your command, scurry backward. This will give you added time to reel in the lead.

"My dog looks so depressed when I call her."

Either you're commanding too harshly or not enthusiastically enough. Use low tones, not cross ones. Also increase your animation; make it seem like more fun. Say "COME," and really run backward or kneel down for the big effect. Never call your dog for something negative.

Ask and Appreciate

Once "COME" is a word your dog associates positively, start encouraging his focus by using it around low-level distractions and increasing the distance from which you call him. Here are some ideas; see whether you can add to the list:

- In front of the TV.
- In the backyard.
- In front of the kids.
- During mealtime.
- In a quiet hallway/garage; attach the Flexi-Leash and increase your distance slowly.

Using the COME command around distractions is a taller order than your living-room version. Most dogs try to pay attention to both the distraction and you at the same time, which anyone who's tried doing two things at once knows is impossible. If your dog's torn, say "NO" and snap the chain when your dog turns towards the distraction. Praise him when he focuses on you. "GOOD DOG!"

Though COME is the command of the day, don't forget to pack each exercise between a couple of normal SIT-STAYs. If you call your dog from each SIT-STAY, he'll start anticipating your request, and since you can't correct a dog that's coming at you, you're stuck. Avoid the problem by working a few SIT-STAYs between each COME command.

The COME command, ask and appreciate. *Andrea Saas.*

THE HUMAN EXPERIMENT

Try calling a human friend, using both methods. First bend over and call to your friend. He'll probably think you've lost a contact lens or something and answer your call rather than come to you. Next, stand up and call. He'll probably come closer.

"I can't get my dog to stop facing distractions."

Ahhh. Stubborn. A hard nut to crack. My advice is to stick with it. Don't lose. You must communicate there's only one way to come and that is to sit directly in front of you. Practice in a quiet room for a day, enthusiastically praising your dog's focus. Next try it with your TV on:

1. Leave her in the STAY.
2. Pause at least a minute (building up her anticipation).
3. With a straight back, deep voice, and gigantic hand signal, call her!
4. Flag her in. If she sits straight, praise her happily!
5. If not, side-step from the distraction and snap the chain firmly, saying "NO."
6. Encourage and praise any focus immediately.

Work up the distraction chain slowly. If she's too stimulated, practice in simpler situations for a while. There's no rush. It's not a race. And whatever you do, don't get frustrated! Frustration kills enthusiasm.

Request and Enforce

The COME command is a funny thing. Used too much, dogs resist it. Think back to the example of someone calling you. If you responded and they had nothing positive to say or do once you got there, you'd be less likely to come the next time they called. If they called every five minutes, you'd probably ignore them after a while or become irritated.

The COME command, request and enforce. *Andrea Saas.*

Dogs are no different. When the day finally arrives when yours understands the COME command, avoid using it all the time. Over-use kills effectiveness. If you want your dog always to respond to "COME," use the command infrequently and make it extremely rewarding! 🐾 *Tip: Don't forget your other commands, too! "INSIDE" when you want your dog to come indoors, "LET'S GO" when you want him to follow you, and "HEEL" when you want him to stay at your side.*

Use the COME command in two of the following situations daily:

- When your dog's distracted on a walk. Regular Teaching or Flexi-Leash.
- Indoors, as your dog's waking up from a nap.
- As your dog's getting out of the car.
- When the neighbor's jogging by.

You can add to the list. Use only two COME commands a day though!

A FUN QUIZ

Look at the following examples, and decide what command you would use in each situation: HEEL, INSIDE or COME.

1. The Good Humor man pulls up across the street. Though you've got no kids and you're a little busy trimming the hedges, half the neighborhood empties onto the street. When your dog starts barking, you command _____ to discourage his focus on the situation.

2. You're walking your dog on his Flexi at the local park. Suddenly, you and your dog notice the same squirrel. You command _____ to bring his focus back to you.

3. Someone arrives at your door asking directions. You command _____ to keep your dog under control, but focused on the situation.

4. It's 11:30 P.M. Your yard is fenced, so you've let your dog out to relieve herself. You use _____ to bring her in.

The correct answers to One and Two is "COME," which tells your dog to stop paying attention to external matters and to focus on you. The answer to Three is "HEEL," which tells your dog to cool it but keeps her involved in the situation. For Four, you would use "INSIDE," a word that means only one thing: When you get your tail in this door, you'll get a treat and a whole lot of loving!

"My dog comes on the Flexi-Leash, but then veers by me."

Are you fudging on the finish? Remember the structure of this command? Your dog must return to you, sit in front of you, and look up. Remind him with a few beginner, six-foot COME exercises. When he's cooperating, go back to your Flexi-Leash and correct him if he races by with "NO" and a leash snap. Bring him into the proper position, and praise as usual.

"My dog looks at me like she's too busy to be bothered."

Kind of amazing to see the thought process. Just tug the leash, say "NO," and encourage her with praise.

"If there's a distraction, my dog will walk sideways and sit on my feet to keep focused on it."

Clever dog. Trying to please everyone. Not exactly what the dog trainer ordered! When your dog takes his eyes off you, sidestep away from the distraction as you snap the lead and say "NO!" Keep sidestepping and snapping until you get through. Don't settle for less than perfection if you're striving for that off-lead response to "COME!"

GAME GALLERY

Training games are a great way to encourage enthusiasm for your commands. I've picked my favorites to share with you.

Game Gallery Index	Command
Demolition Down	DOWN
Four-Footed Fax	GO
Flying Fido	OVER
Hyper Heel	HEEL
Puppy Ping Pong	COME and Personal Names
Ricochet Rover	BRING and OUT
Simon Says "Speak"	SPEAK and QUIET
Sneak-n-Seek	COME
Sniff-n-Snarf	SIT-STAY and HEEL
Snoopy Soccer	LET'S GO
Welcoming Wave	WAVE

Notice the games are listed alphabetically and not necessarily in the order you'll play them. Use them as your dog learns the commands necessary to play.

Demolition Down

This game is super for all those hard-to-get-down dogs out there. It makes the DOWN command gamey and fun. Here's how the game goes:

1. Call your dog over, and ask her to sit down.
2. Brace your legs in a play stance.
3. Dart a short distance across the floor, stop short, and say "SIT."
4. Praise with your voice, and repeat this procedure three times: dart, "SIT," dart, "SIT," dart, "SIT."
5. During your next dart, say "SIT" and suddenly . . .
6. Command "DOWN" as you dive down, slapping the floor with your hands. (If necessary, place your dog calmly. She'll catch on soon.)
7. Release with "OK" and lots of praise!
8. Repeat the SIT sequence and one more DOWN before you quit.

Whew! This game takes a lot out of you.

Four-Footed Fax

"Puppy Ping Pong" and "Ricochet Rover" are prerequisites for this game. I'm sorry to tempt you, but since I've listed them alphabetically, this one comes up first. Once you've mastered those, you can teach your dog to carry important messages to people in your house. Give her a note saying "BRING IT TO MARY." Once your dog has mastered this, you can graduate to other objects. You can send her out for the newspaper (using a command like "BRING ME THE PAPER") or teach her to return those sneakers someone left in the kitchen ("BRING THEM TO BOB"). The recipient should enthusiastically praise a correct delivery.

Flying Fido

This motivational game is fun to practice by yourself or with the kids.

1. Create a low jump by resting a broomstick on two objects of equal height (Rolls of toilet paper or cups make good props).

2. Let your dog sniff the setup before you begin.

3. On a lead, command "OVER" as you jump together.

4. Praise your dog. Make a big thing out of it!

5. Jump back and forth together several times before you quit.

6. After two days, encourage her to take it on her own. Run to the jump, but stop short as you say "OVER!" Praise her, and then call "OVER" as you encourage her back over to your side.

7. Increase the height of the jump as your dog gets the hang of it. Don't push her though; one-and-a-half times the height of your dog's shoulder is the limit.

❀ Note: Puppies need time to develop. If yours is under eight months, keep the jump height below the elbow.

Even kids can play Flying Fido.
Dona Flam.

Hyper Heel

Though you should avoid chasing your dog, as it makes you look like a follower, encouraging her to chase you can be very beneficial. Use this fun time to encourage enthusiasm for the HEEL command. Here's how to play:

1. Pick a favorite toy, and toss it up in the air to get your dog's attention.
2. When she comes over, command "HEEL" and help her into position.
3. Holding the toy in your left hand, say "DAISY, HEEL" and dart forward. (Increase your dart distance as she catches on.)
4. Praise her enthusiastically as she follows you on your left side.
5. As you slow to a stop, help her sit in the Directional Position.
6. Immediately toss her the toy and praise her!

Don't expect perfection, especially at first. You're striving for enthusiasm and fun, and if you get that, you're doing great!

Puppy Ping Pong

This game is a blast! It helps the puppy learn to give a COME response to all family members in addition to teaching your puppy everyone's name. For this fun exercise, you'll need at least two people. In this example, John and Mary are the volunteers.

1. John and Mary stand or sit about ten feet apart.
2. John commands "GO TO MARY" as he points in her direction and withdraws his attention.
3. Mary begins to call "DAISY, COME," praising her as she does.
4. After a few seconds' praise, Mary points "GO TO JOHN" and withdraws her attention.
5. John begins to call "DAISY, COME," praising her as she comes.

After the dog goes back and forth a few times, end the game with hugs from everyone.

🐾 *Note: If your dog is having motivational problems, use toys or treats initially.*

Ricochet Rover

I have to admit I've got a fascination with fetching. The concept of throwing something as far from the body as possible and then having it returned is pretty mind-boggling. First, you'll have to judge whether you can teach this game to your dog. Some dogs love the concept; others will look at you cross-eyed for suggesting such a ludicrous activity. They're all different. If you notice your dog likes to chase and return to you with objects (though he might prefer playing keep-away), try this game:

1. Sit your dog facing you, and show her the ball. If she takes it, praise her. Say "BRING," scratch her head, and act really happy.

2. Next, command "OUT," placing your open palm under her jaw. If your dog does not release the ball, use one of these three approaches:

   a) Prepare five treats on a nearby table. Say "OUT," and place a treat in her mouth. Let the toy drop into your hand. If she's too stimulated by food, try another choice.

   b) Reach your thumb and forefinger around the top of the muzzle behind the canine teeth. Squeeze gently, until the ball is released into your hand.

   c) If your dog knows "OUT" and is being stubborn, snap the lead and say "NO!' Repeat "OUT," then "NO" again if she still resists your request. Repeat this exchange until your dog gives it up. It's a small battle; but once you win, your point will be made and she'll be more agreeable in the future.

3. Once she's cooperating, place her on-lead and toss the ball. Praise her when she makes contact, and command "BRING," reeling her in, if necessary. When she reaches you, say "OUT," enforcing a voluntary release, as described previously.

4. Once this is done, try it on the Flexi-Leash. If she acts up, give it a tug, say "NO," and encourage her good behavior with praise.

Simon Says "Speak"

As anyone who shares his abode with an out-of-control barking dog will tell you, it can be a real headache. Unfortunately, barkers think they're doing the right thing. After all, someone usually starts yelling, which is perceived as barking. In the dog's mind, he alerted the household, whose immediate reaction backs him up. Nightmare potential.

Believe it or not, you can solve this problem with a game. Here's how it goes:

1. Psyche your dog into barking (by ringing a doorbell or standing out of reach)
2. When she starts barking, praise her and say "SPEAK!"
3. For some added encouragement, add a fun hand signal, like snapping your fingers.
4. Let her bark a few times, then say "QUIET" as you offer her a treat.
5. Before trying this in the real world, set up a situation, like the doorbell. When your dog barks, say "SPEAK" as you flash the snappy signal. Next, say "QUIET" as you pop a treat into their mouth and run into another room. Remember, no yelling!

Soon you'll be able to prompt a bark with a snap of your fingers and get your dog to quiet down and come to you willingly! Beautiful.

Sneak-n-Seek

This game helps your dog learn to respond to the COME command. Once a day, do the following:

1. When your dog's in another room, poke your head in the room and say "DAISY, COME!"
2. Run out of sight, clapping your hands and cheering her on.
3. Kneel down, and let her race into you! A sit is not a requirement.

Sniff-n-Snarf

Dogs love this game. In addition to helping them perfect their responses to the STAY and HEEL commands, it teaches them to find things, too. Great when you lose that TV remote!

1. Break a treat into five small pieces. Put them in your pocket.
2. Place your dog in a SIT-STAY.
3. As you let him sniff a treat, say "SNIFF."
4. Remind "STAY" as you place the treat three feet in front of you.
5. Return to his side and pause (varying the duration) as you encourage eye contact.
6. As he's looking up, say "FIND IT!" as you point toward the object.
7. Praise enthusiastically!
8. When he finishes his treat, command "HEEL" to bring him to your side.
9. Repeat five times.

Increase the distance you put the treat in front of you. After you've succeeded at fifteen feet, try hiding the treat around the corner. Your dog will probably act confused; help him out by getting on the floor and acting out a sniff. He'll catch on quickly!

Once he's mastered finding treats, teach him to find other objects. Your keys, for example. Tell him to "SNIFF" them, then place them three feet in front of you. Instruct "FIND IT." When he does, give him a treat. Good boy! By following the preceding sequence, you'll be hiring him out in no time!

Snoopy Soccer

This game doesn't have a specific focus, but it's great fun, and kids love it too. Take a plastic soda liter bottle or milk jug, remove the paper, and put a few Cheerios in the container. (When the Cheerios fall out, it's time to discard the bottle.) Place the bottle down in a clear area of the house, or take your dog outside on her Flexi-Lead. Once your dog's showing some interest, tap the plastic container gently with your foot. After she overcomes her initial caution, you can really have a blast! The only rule is, No hands! This game is especially good if you've got a nippy puppy.

❧ *Note: Never leave your dog alone with plastic objects.*

Welcoming Wave

Is your dog "paw expressive"? Well, it's time to employ those talents. When she is pawing, jump back and say "WAVE!" as you wave your hand in the air frantically. Praise her as she does it! You can use props, like food treats, to encourage the behavior, too. Once you've had enough, say "ENUF!" and ignore her. Soon, your waves will get a quick reply!

Chapter 5

Out and About

I'd say the biggest reward of training is the freedom it gives you to take your dog everywhere! She'll be a welcome social guest, a plus at parades and picnics, and an additional fan at after-school sporting events. In this chapter, we'll cover:

Going public	Entering buildings
Car manners	Curb etiquette
Once you get there	Grates (and other scary objects)
Greeting people	Impressing your veterinarian
Greeting dogs	Going for an overnight visit

GOING PUBLIC

Before that dear dog of yours can accompany you anywhere, you'll need to do some preparatory training. That means going on "practice" runs to selective areas so that you can devote all your attention to your dog. Eventually, it will seem effortless, and your dog will truly be welcome everywhere, but your first trip out may be a real shocker. You'll feel self-conscious, your dog will be too distracted to listen, and you'll feel compelled to tell everyone you see that he's in training. How do I know? I've been there.

Going public.

Are you wondering: "If it's such a nightmare, why bother?" There are three reasons:

1. It gets easier.
2. A well-mannered dog is fun to share.
3. It broadens your dog's focus. You'll be the one looking confident in new, unexplored territories.

Though your first day might be on the chaotic side, it really does get easier. I promise. Keep thinking of the first time you tried something new—driving, tennis, a computer game. It felt awkward initially, right? But if you stuck with it, you're probably an expert by now.

Dog training is the same. The first outing with your perfect-at-home pal may feel more like his first day of training, but don't be discouraged. Think of it as a test to determine whether those house rules apply everywhere. Even I had the first-outing blues with my dog Calvin. As I was trying to steady his HEEL, I walked straight into a light post. Ouch! But that first day passed, and

Calvin learned his manners were expected everywhere, whether greeting Aunt Polly at the door or ten school children in the park. Eventually, the compliments I received on my well-trained dog more than made up for my initial embarrassment, but I didn't start out with perfection, and you may not, either.

So now that you know going public requires some effort, I'd like to help simplify the process, from putting your dog into the car to making the ride home. I'll walk you through it step by step, but before we begin, you should keep in mind some universal rules:

- Keep your dog on-lead. No fancy stuff or showing off. Too many dangers!
- Use lots of encouragement. Cheerfulness is contagious.
- Paws behind heels! Remember: You lead and he follows.
- Keep the communication flowing. Commands provide structure.
- No elimination in public. Take care of that activity at home.
  - 🐾 *Tip: But bring a baggy just in case!*
- Know when to say "NO." To both your dog and other people.

I know, it sounds like a lot. Once you get the hang of this training, though, it'll seem second nature. It's all about leadership. As always. From start to finish. Let's begin!

CAR MANNERS

The first step in shaping your perfect-in-public partner is getting him to the destination with your sanity intact. If some of you are chuckling, it's no wonder. Most dogs are less than cooperative in the car. Jumping from seat to seat and barking at passing strangers is the norm.

To correct this problem, you must think of the situation from your dog's point of view. To him, your automobile is a window box with legs. His own little fishbowl. And while passing cars, pausing for bicycles, and braking for squirrels is part of your normal routine, it pushes his chasing and territorial instincts to their max! Whether he barks or bounces, the predator whizzes away. Conclusion? That he's victorious. The champ! Not only do they run

away, but they run fast! You haven't even gotten out of the car, and your dog's already pumped. See where the problem starts?

First, you need to train your dog or pup to behave. Follow this routine:

1. Lead your dog to the car with the command "HEEL."
2. Open the door, and command "WAIT." Pause.
3. Say "GO TO YOUR SPOT," and direct your dog to a pre-selected area. (See box.)
4. Secure him on a Car Lead, and tell him "STAY."

Now you can proceed. Things always go smoother when they're organized.

A PRESELECTED AREA

As outlined in Chapter 2, pick a car station. It can be in the middle or back area or on the floor of the front passenger seat. Use the place consistently, decorating it with a car lead, blanket and chew toy.

ONCE YOU GET THERE

Getting your dog out of the car calmly is as important as the ride over. Again, from your dog's point of view, the situation is pretty exciting . . . new sights, smells and faces. Don't take it personally if he doesn't notice you or listen to commands at first. Getting him focused is the challenge at hand:

1. Before you open the door, instruct "WAIT."
2. If he jumps forward, catch the car lead, say "NO," and snap back.
3. Re-instruct "WAIT," and pause until he's calm.
4. Put on his Teaching Lead, and say "OK" as you let him exit.
5. Immediately instruct "HEEL," bringing him into the Directional Position, if necessary.
6. Instruct "WAIT" as you shut the door.
7. Proceed with "HEEL."

Now you've arrived! Instantly, your dog will probably have one of two reactions:

If he is a *socialite*, his nose will be twitching a mile a minute, and he'll pivot toward every new stimulation and pull to investigate every blade of grass.

If he is a *shrinking violet* type, the experience may seem overwhelming. His tail may disappear, his body may lower, and, when stimulated, he may try to hide behind you.

Neither situation is good nor permissible, but this is what you can expect. If you follow your Socialite or bend to soothe your Shrinking Violet, you'll be reinforcing the dog's reaction by following his lead. And since I can't let you do that, I've come up with a better plan.

BE AWARE!

Be prepared to attract some attention when you go out training. Some people, like myself, delight in dogs and love to talk to people who share the same passion. If people ask to pet your dog and you don't feel ready to handle the situation, you can reply politely: "Thank you for asking. I've just begun training though, and we're not ready yet. Catch us in a week or two!"

For your Socialite: Enforcing the HEEL command is paramount. Telling strangers to back off until he's trained is a must. Embarrassing I know, but a must. (You don't want him jumping up and giving someone a scratch, even by accident). You must be stern in your efforts and clear in your commands. If you ask for a SIT-STAY, get a SIT-STAY. Take all commands back to the introductory stage, no matter how well you're doing at home. Initially, practice only HEEL and STAY commands.

For your Shrinking Violet: It's so tempting to soothe. You've got to keep reminding yourself that your dog is not human. Say it to yourself over and over: Soothing reinforces fear, soothing reinforces fear. Instead, do the following:

1. Look confident, and stand tall like a good leader dog. Soon, he'll mimic you!
2. Bring some treats and a favorite toy along to focus his attention outward. Withholding them at home makes the new adventure seem really exciting!
3. Use the HEEL and STAY commands often; familiar sounds soothe anxiety.
4. If he's too nervous to listen, enforce a response without corrections.
5. Stay calm and positive. Deflect any admirers until he's feeling more safe.

"Heel! Are you joking? He does it great at home, but he's a maniac everywhere else!"

There are two remedies for an out-of-control HEEL:

The Sidestep: Whenever your dog is focusing on something to your left, take a giant step to the right, snap the lead, and remind him: "HEEL." The bigger or older the dog, the sharper the snap. Repeat and repeat until your dog's alerting to you. Praise that!

The Kick Back: If you've got a charging brute on your hands, lock your left hand to the back of your thigh. The second he moves forward, remind "HEEL" as you thrust your left leg back. Don't kick him, though; just move your leg in the opposite direction as you remind "HEEL." Repeat and repeat until he stays behind your leg.

If you're still having problems, consider using a different collar or try holding the lead behind your back.

"My dog starts barking the second I let him out of the car!"

A very excited guy. On your first trips out, practice in the back of an empty parking lot. Tote along a travel mister pump, which you can find at your local pharmacy, filled with white vinegar. If he should start barking, spritz his nose and say "SSHHH." You must be sneaky about the spritz though, because you don't want him to know where it is coming from. Purchase a travel mister small enough to hide in your hand.

> *"My dog's so afraid, she freezes and won't move. I've never seen her this bad."*

If she's terrified, get some help. Try coaxing her forward with her favorite treats and praise, but if she refuses to eat, follow my first suggestion.

GREETING PEOPLE

Stop shaking. This doesn't have to be a hair-raising experience. Just keep your head on straight, and remember everything I've taught you. I have faith in you!

Before I talk you through the procedure though, please read over the following disclosures. If you identify with any of them, please follow my specific instructions and skip the rest of this section.

First Disclosure: If your dog is having aggression problems, the only person you must introduce your dog to is a trainer with a specialty in

Dream control!

aggression rehabilitation. How do you find such an expert? Ask your veterinarian. It's better to be safe than sued.

Second Disclosure: If you notice your dog getting nervous or tense around unfamiliar people, join a class or work under private supervision. Don't push the issue alone.

Third Disclosure: If you don't believe the training will work, it won't. Hire some extra help to build your own confidence!

If you're still with me, here are five key rules to follow when debuting that dog of yours:

Rule #1: Make sure your dog is familiarized and comfortable with the setting before attempting to share him with anyone. Don't greet people your first day out!

Rule #2: Feet ahead of paws! Correct all attempts to scootch forward.

Rule #3: Tell admirers what you're doing. "We're in training."

Rule #4: Stay more focused on your dog than on any admirers. Correct all attempts to break.

Rule #5: Put faith in your own knowledge. Just because everyone has advice doesn't mean it's right. "I don't mind if he jumps" doesn't hold water. You mind. Period.

Now for the actual greeting. Drum roll, please! How you handle the situation will depend on none other than your dog. If yours is overly enthusiastic, you'll need to tame her expressiveness. Keeping her focused on you is the key.

HANDLING THE SOCIALITES

1. Ask people to wait until she's calm.
2. Enforce a SIT-STAY, keeping your feet ahead of her paws.
3. Place your left hand, fingers down, along her waist and below the ribs.
4. Using your right thumb to brace her collar, hold her steady should she jump.
5. If the person still wants to, he or she can pet your dog!
6. Remind "STAY," and don't let up your vigil until the person is gone.
7. Remember, for this to happen automatically, you must teach it first.

Whew—what a workout!

If your dog is more passive in his approach to new people, try this approach:

HANDLING THE SHRINKING VIOLETS

1. Ask your greeter to wait until you and your dog are in position.
2. Place your dog in a SIT-STAY, and kneel down at his side.
3. Put your left hand on his waist and your right hand under his chest.
4. Hold his head up for confidence as you and the greeter pet and praise him.

Soon, his reaction will be automatic, too!

"My dog's more sensitive to men than to women. Sometimes he growls at them."

This problem results from any number of circumstances. Generally, all are due to either inappropriate or lack of socialization with men. Whatever the cause, make sure that you use your dog's favorite treats for the introduction. Try this approach:

1. Instruct your man friend to avoid direct eye contact with your dog.
2. Do not force the situation. Act cheerful and cordial to the man, setting a good example.
3. Casually place a treat on the man's foot, and praise your dog if he takes it.
4. Ask the man to kneel calmly while continuing to avoid direct eye contact.
5. Offer the man some treats to hold, and praise your dog if he takes them from the man.
6. The man should continue to offer your dog fistfuls of treats as he get calmer.
7. Eventually, when your dog initiates the interaction, try petting him together.

🐾 *Note: If the man is visiting your home, place your dog on his Teaching Lead during arrivals and follow the same directions.*

If the problem doesn't improve, seek professional help.

"My dog is suspicious of children, and my husband and I are planning to have kids. What can I do?"

If the problem doesn't improve with the following suggestions, find a private trainer who has experience with this problem. To socialize your dog with children, try this:

1. Practice your HEEL and SIT-STAY patterns around the perimeter of a playground. Do not let the children approach.
2. Act like children with your dog. For example, poke him or pull his ear like a child would do, squeal in high-pitched voices, and stare at him at his level by kneeling or crawling. Once he's socialized to these patterns, he'll be more accepting when the children do it. If your dog's nervous of babies, borrow a friend's blanket (for the aroma) and wrap a doll baby in it to carry around the house, including your dog in all the fuss!
3. Condition him to the sound of his treat box, and take it with you when you'll be around kids. Let the kids take the box and toss treats to your dog. If he's enthusiastic, you can let him take treats gently from the children.

Note: If your dog tenses up, his eyes grow cold, or he starts to growl, do not work him around children until you are under the supervision of a professional trainer. You don't want you and your dog to be another statistic. Dogs who bite children are often forcibly euthanised.

GREETING DOGS

Are you shaking again? Envisioning your dog hurling himself at the end of the lead? Well, wake up! You're having a nightmare.

Seriously, though. If you've had some stressful encounters in the past, try to put them behind you. Memories cloud control. Wipe the slate clean, and have faith in what I've taught you. If you see a dog when you're out and about, don't approach the dog immediately. First, get control of your situation:

1. If your dog acts stimulated, snap the lead firmly and remind "HEEL."
2. Continue in your original direction, and pick up your pace.
3. Don't look toward, approach or follow the other dog.
4. If your dog continues her shenanigans, speed up and keep snapping. *Remember: Keep her behind you!*
5. Praise her for focusing on you. *Don't give in or let up!*

Once you have your dog under control, you can permit a greeting by saying "OK, GO PLAY!" Before you do, though, make certain the other dog is friendly and the other owner is respectful of your training efforts. When playtime is over, instruct your dog back to the HEEL position and move on.

"What if someone approaches me?"

If you're not in the mood or your dog's too hyped, just say "NO." If you're game, however, get your dog in control behind you, then release him with an "OK, GO PLAY!" Call him back to the HEEL position when playtime is over.

"What if we're approached by an aggressive, off-lead dog?"

I love this question. When approached by an aggressive dog, do not turn or make eye contact, and prevent your dog from doing the same. Correct any confrontational attempts your dog makes as you hightail it from the scene. The aggressive dog is protecting what he considers to be his territory. If you leave without confronting him, he'll stop the chase immediately to harbor his fighting reserves for a more threatening foe.

ENTERING BUILDINGS

Pick a building you might visit with your dog: the veterinarian's office, a hardware store, a pet shop, your kid's school. Your dog's behavior in those buildings will depend on one major factor. Can you guess it? It will depend on who enters the building first. Yup, that's it. If your dog leads you, than he's in charge. If you lead your dog, than you're the head honcho. The Leader. And whoever starts in charge, stays in charge.

Taking for granted that you're going to run the show, let's pick up the situation following your exit from the car. You've just brought your dog into a HEEL position. Continuing to walk in this manner, you approach the building:

1. As you get to the threshold, brace your arm behind your back. (Dogs sense when they're going somewhere new!)
2. Say "SSHHH" if he starts getting excited.
3. Pause before you open the door, and command "WAIT."
4. Don't open the door until he's settled down.
5. Re-command "WAIT" as you open the door.
6. If your dog lunges, snap him back sternly and say "NO!"
7. Pause again until your dog is calm.
8. Then say "OK" as you lead him through!

"My dog is cautious when entering new buildings."

You may be unconsciously reinforcing her anxiety. Remember, if your dog's showing fear, you must show confidence. No petting or reassuring her it will "BE OK." Instead, take along some treats to encourage her as you approach the building. Stand tall, and ignore her trepidation. If she puts on the breaks, kneel down to encourage her forward. If you can, bring a friend along to help coach her inside.

CURB ETIQUETTE

Whether you live in Manhattan or not, eventually you'll run across a curb. Applying our usual psychology, some restraint is in order here!

1. As you approach the curb, your dog should be in a HEEL position.
2. At the curb, instruct "WAIT."

Curb etiquette in action.

3. If your dog continues moving forward, snap the lead and say "NO, WAIT," pulling him behind your ankles.
4. Say "OK" as you lead him across.
5. Remind "HEEL."

"Should I instruct a SIT-STAY if we're forced to wait?"

That's up to you. If your dog is fidgety, then, definitely, yes. The SIT-STAY is very grounding. Good application!

GRATES (AND OTHER SCARY OBJECTS)

Dogs see the world a little differently than we do. Take your average grate, for example. Standing five feet above it, we see it as pretty harmless because our binocular vision can separate the spaces from the bars. To a dog, who would never see such things in the wild, the grate looks pretty scary! Having little depth perception, dogs see the holes more like an abyss.

Bearing that in mind, also remember that your dog is a very habitual creature. At home, she comforts in consistencies. Whenever alerted to a new obstacle, even a new piece of furniture, her sense of stability is thrown. If you've ever seen this, you've probably noticed a cautious stance, worried eyes, an avoid-approach pattern, and eventually a full-length-stretch-to-sniff investigation. After a couple of days, if the furniture remained stationary, the dog would accept it as normal.

When you go out, you may run into objects or obstacles that may have the same effect on your dog. How you handle the situation will determine the tone of your dog's reaction. If you try to calm her, your body language and voice will be communicating fear, and she'll grow more and more wary.

On the other hand, if you act confident by investigating the new object on your own, you'll highlight your courage and impress your dog. She'll follow your lead and, after seeing no harm come to you, will grow more confident in you.

One fall evening, I was walking my dog Calvin when suddenly we came upon some leaf bags blowing in the wind. Mr. Confidence himself suddenly crouched in fear, ran behind my legs, and started woofing at the unusual sight. Instead of petting him, I let the lead go slack and walked forward to investigate the bags by myself. Slowly he crept up, paused, stretched his body long with his nose extended, and then pounced on the bags as if to say "I wasn't afraid of these dumb old bags anyway!"

"My dog refuses to walk over grates."

Take you dog's favorite treats, and go sit on a grate. Encourage him to the perimeter. Slowly bait him forward, and praise him as he attempts his first steps. It may take weeks to see him walk over a grate calmly, but your efforts will be worth the reward.

"My five-month-old puppy has developed a fear of people in uniform."

Helping to overcome a dog's fears.

I can relate to that. I still get a little nervous about uniforms myself! To help him overcome his fear, act very friendly toward uniformed people. Ask them to help you socialize your puppy as you give them some treats to offer him. If they're willing, ask them to kneel and avoid eye contact until he's sniffed them out. Another great trick is to rent a uniform from a costume shop and dress up in one yourself!

IMPRESSING YOUR VETERINARIAN

I'll let you in on a secret. Veterinarians love a well-behaved dog. It makes their job a lot easier. To impress yours, do the following:

1. Bring your dog's favorite chew in case you've got to wait. (When you get to the office, your dog will probably be excited or afraid.)
2. Instruct "HEEL" at the car, and command "WAIT" at the entrance.
3. Say "OK," and remind "HEEL" as you check in.

PUPS AND STAIRS

One of the cutest miracles I get to perform is teaching pups to handle stairs. I'll tell you my secret. Once your puppy is large enough to make it downstairs, avoid carrying him. Instead, brace his rib cage securely in your hands and help him to manipulate his body to do the action. Don't forget to praise him while you do. If yours is really frightened by the whole flight, carry him to the bottom few stairs and ask someone to kneel below to coach him forward.

4. If you must wait, place him in a TOWN DOWN, under your legs, and give him his favorite chew.
5. Instruct "WAIT" as you go into the examination room together to keep him calm and focused!

"My dog is very suspicious of receptionists and growls whenever one approached her."

Set up a practice run, and ask the receptionist to meet you outside. Give her your treat box, and ask her to kneel without making eye contact with your dog. When your dog approaches, have the receptionist reward her with treats. Repeat this procedure at the threshold of the office and once more inside.

"My dog gets on the seat next to me and looks threateningly at everyone who passes."

What is he doing on the seat? He's not a person. By letting him sit at your level, you're encouraging him to assume a protective roll. Instead, put him in a TOWN DOWN and ignore him. If he growls, tell him "NO." If you're still having problems, refer to Chapter 7.

GOING FOR AN OVERNIGHT VISIT

Taking your dog with you on an overnight visit can be a lot of fun. Or it can be a nightmare. It's all in how you handle the situation. Here are some suggestions.

Do some pre-departure planning. Pack your dog's favorite sleeping blanket or bed, and his crate; and tuck in his favorite chew toys, the props for a familiar game (soda bottle or ball), treats, his Flexi-Leash, and a small portable radio. Yes, a radio; it drowns out any unfamiliar sounds and soothes his anxiety while you're out.

When you arrive, if you're going to do any heavy greeting, leave your dog in the car with the radio playing. Overly enthusiastic hellos can start things off on the wrong note.

Bring your dog into the situation on his Teaching Lead. Enforce a SIT for greetings and a WAIT at all thresholds.

Go to your room, and set up his crate and sleeping station, while you give him some treats and a chew toy. Then set up the radio next to his crate.

If possible, avoid crating immediately. After setting up the bedroom, walk around the outside perimeters and play a familiar game.

When you must leave him, place him in his crate calmly with a chew toy and turn on the radio. (Make sure you depart calmly (no overly theatrical guilt-trip scenes, please) and arrive in the same fashion. *Tip: When you turn on the radio, try to find a classical station. Heavy Metal can be a little jarring!*

"My friends have two dogs. How should we introduce them?"

If your friend will agree, let the introduction take place at a neutral location, such as an empty playground or a field. Otherwise, meet outside the house in a yard or on a sidewalk. This prevents a fierce territorial reaction. When they first meet, you should expect a lot of threat bluffs, such as growling, mouthiness and mounting. It's natural, so don't overreact; your interference might prompt a fight. Stay calm and observe closely. The dogs must determine a hierarchy, and once that's accomplished they'll settle down. If you're certain a fight has begun, separate them with the leashes or a bucket of water. Don't handle fighting dogs.

"We are staying at my in-laws, and they have two young children. What's the best way to introduce my dog?"

Before you go, take a box of Cheerios, shake it, and toss your dog a handful. Repeat this activity until she recognizes the sound. Tell your in-laws to have an identical box waiting for your arrival. Let your dog check the place out when you first get there; then encourage the children, or the parent with the child, to shake the box. Offer fistfuls as your dog is first introduced to the new smells and stimulation involved with young kids. Praise her as she explores. 🐾 *Tip: If you anticipate or sense any aggression, do not socialize your dog with the children. Seek professional help immediately!*

"My dog barks every time I'm out of sight."

Poor thing. He's frightened. Whatever you do, avoid discipline as it will heighten his fear. Next, try a quick obedience session. If all is going well, instruct "STAY" and dart out of sight for a few seconds. Return quickly and praise. Next, try stationing him with a familiar blanket and toy, and tell him "WAIT" as you leave for the bathroom. If you come back to an anxious dog, ignore him until he settles down. When he does, praise him warmly and offer a treat. Continue making short departures until he stays calm.

When you must leave, contain him with familiar toys and blankets, and don't forget the radio. If he's anxious when you return, ignore him until he's calm. It will only take a minute or two, I promise!

Chapter 6

Your Off-Lead Companion

Having a well-trained off-lead dog is definitely all it's cracked up to be. In this chapter, you'll learn how to:

Steady an off-lead STAY
Get your dog's focus at a distance
Teach and use an Emergency DOWN
Work all commands off-lead, including COME

In Chapter 5, we went over leash-training techniques. Please make sure you've mastered them before you begin the exercises outlined in this chapter. As we work toward off-lead control, keep your dog in a confined area. She may get distracted at first and ignore you, not out of spite but excitement. If you fall into the trap of chasing or correcting your dog, she may remain unfooled by or skeptical of your off-lead control forever.

Before we begin, add the following items to your equipment collection:

- *The Flexi-Leash:* This retractable leash is invaluable for advanced work. The longer, the better.
- *The Twenty-Foot Tree Line:* You will be attaching this line to a tree to practice long-distance command control. Purchase a canvas leash, or make your own out of a clothesline and a clip.

- *The Thirty-Foot Long Line:* You'll be using this for distance control with the WAIT, HEEL, DOWN and COME commands. Purchase a canvas lead, or use a clothesline.
- *The Ten-Foot Line:* Make this in the same fashion as the thirty-foot line. You'll use this line to reinforce your control in the house.
- *The Short Lead:* This training tool should be long enough to grab but short enough not to distract your dog.

❧ *Note: Attach all lines to your dog's buckle collar, not her training collar. Place three knots in your lines at equal distances to allow for a quick grab if your dog should dart away.*

As you work through the following exercises, keep these three suggestions in mind:

1. *Detach:* When you first start weaning off-lead, you may feel like you're working with an untrained dog. Don't get disheartened. It's natural for

YOUR MIND SET

Training off-lead takes a lot of concentration, self-control and focus. And I'm not just talking about your dog! The toughest thing to discipline during this process isn't your dog, it's your temper. We humans are a control-oriented bunch. We want our dogs to come when called, stay calm in exciting situations, and control their fun-loving "gamey" impulses. But off-lead, dogs think "play, explore, chase!" They are either terrified or unimpressed by human frustration. To train your dog properly, you must first see the situation from her eyes. By understanding her perspective, you'll be able to perk up the following exercises to encourage her participation. Knowing when to animate your exercises versus when to stand firm, you'll have an off-lead dog in no time!

her to test you a little, so avoid taking it personally. I know, this is more a meditation exercise than a dog-training technique, but if you show your frustration, you'll look weak. So stay cool. Detach. Though you may think all your training has been a waste of time, it hasn't.

2. *Watch that eye contact:* Eye contact communicates control. If your dog can get you to look to her more than you can get her to look to you, then guess what? When the leash is gone, you're the follower. To avoid this disaster, make sure you work in a confined area so that you can ignore your dog when she disobeys or tries to get your attention. If you're near a house, walk inside. A graceful retreat is not a failure.

3. *Fall back:* Even if you've successfully weaned your dog off the Teaching Lead, don't hesitate to use it when your dog is over-stimulated, unable to focus, or disobeying her basic commands. For example, don't be embarrassed to leash your dog if she's still rusty when company visits. Using it helps control the situation while simultaneously conditioning more appropriate behavior.

NEW EQUIPMENT FOR LEARNING RIGHT

Off-lead dogs aren't created overnight. Like everything else, it's a step-by-step process. You'll be using your new equipment to increase your dog's focus, but don't get itchy fingers. Just because she behaves well on her Flexi-Leash one day doesn't mean she's ready for an off-lead romp the next. Take your time. Gradual. Step by step.

Though each piece of equipment will be explained separately, you should use them interchangeably.

The Flexi-Leash

This leash is a great exercising tool. It allows your dog freedom to explore while still leaving you in complete control. As a training tool, you can use it informally during walks to reinforce the following commands:

A Flexi-Leash is an invaluable tool for your off-lead
aspirations.

NAME   Call out your dog's name enthusiastically: "DAISY!" If she looks
to you, praise her. That's all that's required. Just a glance. If she ignores you,
snap the leash; then praise her once you've got her attention.

WAIT   Use this command to make your dog stop three feet in front of you.
If your dog continues forward, snap the leash and say "NO, WAIT." Increase
the distance in front of you to six, eight, twelve, sixteen and twenty-six feet.

SIT-STAY   The Flexi-Leash enables you to increase your distance control.
As the Flexi will add resistance to the collar, practice the Tug Test before you
walk out. Increase your distance incrementally.

HEEL   Use this command to call your dog back to your side. Call out her
name, and then command "HEEL" as you slap your leg. Praise your dog as
she responds; then walk a short distance before you stop to release her.

EMERGENCY DOWN   This exercise can be a real lifesaver, but don't practice it before your dog has mastered the DOWN command.

1. Stand next to your unsuspecting dog.
2. Suddenly command "DOWN" in a very life-threatening tone (the type
   of tone you'd use if a loved one were about to walk off a cliff).
3. Kneel down quickly as you bring your dog into position.
4. Act like you're being bombed, too.

Soon, your dog will catch on and act independently. Once she does, begin extending your distance from her. This exercise could save your dog's life if you were ever separated by an on-coming vehicle.

🐾 *Note: This exercise is very stressful! Limit your practice to two sessions of three Emergency DOWN sequences weekly.*

NO   Whenever your dog's focusing on something she shouldn't, snap the leash and say "NO!" Immediately refocus her attention with a toy, stick or another command.

A REAL LIFESAVER

It's true! The Emergency DOWN really does saves lives. Even I have a story to tell. Once I was leaving my training classes with my Husky, Kyia, when a tennis ball slipped loose and started rolling toward the road. Kyia, sweet thing, wanted to help and ran innocently to collect it. In a panic, I shouted "DOWN," and she dropped like she'd been shot. What a good girl. She got a few extra biscuits for the car ride home!

The Ten-Foot Line

Place the ten-foot line on your dog when she's indoors and you can watch her. Every couple of minutes, stand by the line and give a command (SIT, DOWN, WAIT, COME). If she looks confused, step on the line and say "NO" calmly. Re-command enthusiastically, and help her into position. For example, if you command "DOWN" and she gives you a blank stare, say "NO" and re-command as you guide her into position. Always praise your dog regardless of her initial cooperation. Your understanding will help her overcome her off-lead confusion.

Use your ten-foot line to enforce your
indoor control.

:paw: *Note: If your dog gives you some defiant canine back-talk (a bark or dodge), step on the lead, snap it firmly as you say "NO," and station and ignore her for fifteen minutes. She's been grounded with no TV.*

The Short Lead

Once your dog is responding to the ten-foot line, progress to the short lead. Attach it to your dog's buckle collar, and use it to reinforce the stationary commands SIT, STAY, DOWN and WAIT, and the proper positioning for HEEL and COME.

Three times a week, bring your dog into a quiet room and practice a command routine. Initially, hold the short lead, but then drop it once you've warmed up. Slap your leg, and use hand signals and peppy body language to encourage your dog's focus.

Your short lead will be a reminder
for your dog and provide quick
reinforcement.

The Twenty-Foot Tree Line

Tie this line to a tree or post. Please make all knots secure. Leave the line on the ground, and follow this sequence:

1. Warm up with five minutes of regular on-lead practice. Stop your dog next to the line, and attach it discreetly to your dog's buckle collar.
2. Remove her regular lead, and place it on the ground in front of her. Keep your hands free.
3. Command "STAY," and walk out ten feet. Extend your distance as she gains control.
4. Run your fingers through your hair, and swing your arms gently back and forth to emphasize that your dog is off-lead.
5. If she falls for this and darts for a quick getaway, wait until she's about to hit the end of the line to shout "NO!" Return her back into position, and repeat the exercise at closer range.

Tree lines improve focus and long-distance corrections.

6. As your dog improves, practice an out-of-sight SIT-STAY.
7. Practice DOWN from a SIT-STAY and a DOWN-STAY.
8. You can also practice the COME command, but never call at a distance greater than the line will reach.

If your dog disobeys, determine whether her response is motivated by anxiety or confusion, or defiance. If she's confused or anxious, do not issue a correction. Calmly return to her side and reposition gently. Repeat the same exercise at close range. If your dog breaks defiantly, however, either shout "NO" as she hits the end of the line; or, if she's baiting you, return quietly and snap the lead as you say "NO." Re-position, and repeat the exercise at close range for quicker control. Good luck!

The Thirty-Foot Long Line

In an enclosed outdoor area, attach your dog to the thirty-foot long line and allow her to roam freely under your supervision. Engage her by playing with a stick or ball, and investigate the surroundings together. Avoid over-commanding. Just hang out and enjoy some free time with your dog.

Every five minutes, position yourself near the line and issue a command enthusiastically.

If it's a stationary command, like SIT, WAIT or DOWN, stop abruptly and stamp your foot with the command and signal. If it's a motion command like COME or HEEL, run backward as you encourage your dog toward you. If she races over, help her into the proper position and give her a big hug. If your dog ignores your command, quickly step on the line and say "NO." Don't scream, just speak sternly. After your correction, give your dog the opportunity to right her reaction before lifting the line to snap it or reeling her in. End your session with a favorite game.

Wrap-up

Remember, as you work through these exercises with your dog, she's trying to read and anticipate your behavior as you try to anticipate hers. Think for a minute. If I were to ask your dog to describe you, what would she say? "Fun to be around, happy, confident and in control." Or would she say "Impatient, scary to get close to when I'm off-lead, easily fooled and unsure." Your dog has an opinion and responds to you accordingly. Make a good impression. Stand tall, command confidently, and don't be afraid to have a little fun! That's what having an off-lead dog is all about!

"When will I know that I can trust my dog off-lead?"

You should feel it. It's usually not a smooth road in the beginning; some days you'll get a quick and happy response, others will feel more like your first day of training. Stay cool, though. Frustration is a sign of weakness and will lessen your control. Keep your dog enclosed as you practice so that if she starts to act cocky, you can retreat immediately. And don't hesitate to go back to Long-Line or Teaching Lead exercises for quick review.

❖ *Note: Do not allow your dog off-lead in an unconfined area.*

"It's so frustrating when my dog ignores me. I feel like I'm going to explode. I want to hit him."

Feeling like hitting something is fine. Hitting your dog isn't. It would erode your relationship and diminish his off-lead trust. If you're really angry, walk away calmly. Remember: Retreat is not failure.

"Can I use treats for the off-lead stuff?"

I don't recommend it. Treats become very addictive and, as you'd soon find out, dogs taught with food are less responsive when it's not around. Training should focus your dog on you, so make yourself the treat! ❧ *Tip: How do you make yourself the treat? By giving your dog enough praise and interacting with him so much that he loves to be with and obey you.*

"My dog breaks everytime I leave him in a SIT-STAY on his Flexi-Leash."

Did you practice the Tug Test? Once you've done that, increase your distance slowly. For example, if your dog breaks every time you walk out fifteen feet, then practice at ten feet for a week. Gradually move up to eleven feet, twelve feet, etc. In addition, don't face your dog as you walk out. Walking backward invites a COME response. Instead, walk out confidently, back toward your dog, and pivot at your final destination. Remind "STAY."

"Don't the lines get caught around trees and doors?"

Yes they do. Clip all lines to the buckle collar, and never leave your dog unsupervised.

"When I shout NO on the tree line, my dog crouches down and barks at me. I find it hard not to laugh."

Don't laugh! You'll be undermining your efforts and teaching your dog that when the lead comes off, the games begin. Instead, stand still by your dog, but completely ignore her. Wait until she's through with her silly display; then return her to the original position, and repeat an easier version of the same exercise. If she just won't quit, place her on her Teaching Lead, and do some beginner exercises before calling it a day.

"When I go to position my dog, she stays just out of reach."

Watch that body language and negative eye contact. Being off the Teaching Lead is as nerve-wracking for her as it is for you. Look at the ground as you return to your dog. If she's still out of reach, kneel down and wait. When she approaches, take her collar gently, reposition, and work at close range.

"My dog picks the end of the line up in her mouth and prances around me like a show horse."

Clever girl. Try soaking the end of the line in Bitter Apple liquid or Tabasco sauce overnight. If she's still acting cocky, quietly go inside and watch her discreetly from the window.

"When I place my dog on the short lead, I can't get near her."

You'll need to work on your ten-foot line for another week or so. When you try the short lead again, place it on with your ten-foot line and correct her by stepping on it when she darts away.

Chapter 7

The Encyclopedia of Canine Etiquette

Aggression

Barking

Chasing

Chewing

Digging

Garbage Grabbing

Housebreaking

Inedible Ingestion (*pica*)

Jumping

Mounting

Nipping/Mouthing

Separation Anxiety

Stimulated Sprinkling

Stool Swallowing (*Coprophagia*)

Timidity

Many of the following solutions to these problems use techniques from Chapters 1 through 3. Please read them if you haven't already. As you work to solve your problems, remember that few dogs consider their behavior bad. Though you may argue that your dog "knows what he's done wrong," anyone, dog or human, would look frightened if you screamed at him. Don't confuse fear with comprehension. Most bad behavior is a reaction to attention and not understanding what is expected.

AGGRESSION

This section deals with the many forms of aggression. It is a serious and sober topic. If you're having a problem, get help. Seek a well-known and respected behaviorist or trainer in your area. Your veterinarian may be of help finding one. My recommendations are just that, recommendations. Do not follow them if you are unsure whether they apply to your situation. *Aggression, if approached incorrectly or with caution or fear, can result in a serious bite.*

Though people are embarrassed to admit to it, most dogs show aggression in some situations, whether with their owners, strangers, other dogs or furry little tidbits running around the backyard. If you're dealing with an aggression problem, you're not alone. Aggression is a normal form of canine communication, similar to our anger. Often it is seen in dogs who as puppies were dominant and bossy and not given the proper instruction from their owners. An example is the spoiled dog who is given too much attention. This dog thinks his owners depend on him for leadership. After all, they act like servants. When that owner tries to direct his dog or discipline him in a stimulated situation, the dog sees the owner as acting out of line and thinks he must reprimand him, as if he were a delinquent child. Since dogs can't send naughty owners to their room, they snap, growl or bite. Same concept, different communication. This however, is not the only type of aggression. It comes in many other forms. The next sections describe the eight categories of aggression.

Dominant Aggression

The potential for developing this type of aggression can usually be seen in puppyhood. An active pup who steals clothing for fun, barks for attention, leans against his owners when in new environments or around strangers, or who successfully solicits attention whenever the mood strikes, is dominant. Though the aggression may not surface, all too often it does. And when it does, the problem lies not with the dog, who thinks its leadership qualities are appreciated, but with the owners, who must now assert themselves to solve the problem.

Spatial Aggression

A dog who shows aggression while eating or sleeping or being groomed or cared for by a family member, stranger or other dog professional (veterinarian or groomer) is showing spatial aggression. It is usually tied in with dominant, territorial or psychotic aggression.

Territorial Aggression

Dogs who act threatening only when strangers approach their home turf are territorial. This problem is encouraged by the following:

- When delivery people approach and leave the home territory, the dog thinks that he drove them away, and his aggression is reinforced.
- When the owners are home and react to a territorial response by yelling or physical handling, the dog can't understand this as discipline and concludes that the situation must be very suspicious for his owners to react this way. Their reaction reinforces aggression.
- When a dog reacts aggressively in a car or on a tie-out, he is warning all intruders to stay away. Since they do, he considers himself victorious and his territorial aggression is reinforced.
- When dogs are isolated during greetings or visits, they may develop Frustrated Territorial Aggression (FTA). It's not good. You see, in a normal group of dogs, the leader would permit or deny entry to a visitor, who is then "sniffed out" by the rest of the pack. Isolation frustrates this normal process and will encourage a more assertive response the next time the doorbell rings. While guard and herding dogs are more commonly known for this type of aggression (again, detectable in puppyhood), it can be seen in any breed.

Protective Aggression

This dog thinks his job is to protect his owner. Even off his territory, this dog will react aggressively if anyone approaches. It is not uncommon for dogs to develop this sort of relationship with a young child or a passive, inexperienced owner. The owner—man, woman or child—is perceived as weak and in need of protection.

Predatory Aggression

This is another instinctive behavior from ancestral times when dogs were wolves and hunted for survival. Although we have suppressed the drive to kill in most breeds, some—Nordic and terriers especially—still kill innately.

Fear-Induced Aggression

In every litter, there will be shy puppies. Mama's boys (or girls) who depend on her wisdom for safety. In human homes, these dogs continue their dependency needs. Their timidity, which surfaces in new situations, may turn to overwhelming fear if they're not given proper direction and support from their owners. A dog in this situation may react aggressively. Although shyness is a temperamental trait, there is also a learned element to the behavior. When an owner attempts to soothe a frightened dog, the attention reinforces the fear. Additionally, when strangers or caring professionals back away from a threatening dog, the take-home message is that aggression works!

Dog-to-Dog Aggression

Aggression between dogs occurs when they perceive their territories as overlapping (this can happen anywhere, as some dogs think their territory is very extensive) or when there is a hierarchial struggle in a multi-dog household. It is often exaggerated by well-meaning owners who scream or pull back when their dog is showing aggression. This only adds to the tension.

Psychotic Aggression

It's very rare that I come across a psychotic dog or puppy, but they do exist, and for me not to address the issue would be irresponsible. Most, though not all, are the result of poor breeding. This problem is identified by erratic or fearful aggression responses in very atypical situations, which can often be traced back to early puppyhood. There are two categories:

- *Erratic Viciousness:* At unpredictable intervals, this dog/puppy will growl fiercely from his belly. It may happen when his owner passes his food bowl, approaches when he's chewing a toy, or even walks by him. At other times, the dog is perfectly sweet. A "Jekyll and Hyde" personality.

- *Fear Biters:* These dogs show dramatic fear or a startled bite response to non-threatening situations such as their owner turning a page of the newspaper or moving an arm suddenly. They can act extremely confused or threatened when strangers approach.

❧ *Note: Many well-educated dog people use the term "fear biter" incorrectly. There is a big difference between a dog/puppy who bites out of fear and a fear biter. Don't automatically assume the worst if someone labels your dog with this term.*

Please don't panic if your dog occasionally growls at you or barks at the mailman. A lot of dogs/puppies growl when protecting a food dish or toy, and the guarding instinct is strong in many breeds. These behavioral problems can be cured or controlled with proper training. Many biters can be rehabilitated. The situations I'm speaking of involve severe aggression: bared teeth, hard eyes, a growl that begins in the belly, and a bite response you'd expect from a trained police dog. These personality disturbances are seen very early, usually by four months of age.

It's both frightening and tragic because nothing can be done to alter their development. If you suspect that your puppy might have either of these abnormalities, speak to your breeder and veterinarian immediately, and call a specialist to analyze the situation. These dogs must be euthanised. In my career, I've seen only six cases, and all were purchased from unknown or suspect breeders.

What to Do about Different Types of Aggression

I specialize in rehabilitating aggression, and nothing gives me more pleasure then to see a situation resolved. If you have an aggressive dog, the first thing you must do is consult a professional in your area. Immediately. The dog world does not need another bite on the record books. Next, keep your dog off your bed. This is a big deal. If you've got an aggressive dog, he thinks it's his duty to protect or keep you in line. The first step in resolving this issue is to take over the high sleeping grounds. Tie your dog to your dresser if you

THE SHAKER-BOX The best shaker-boxes contain your dog's favorite treats. If your dog loves Milk Bones, use them. I know one who had a fetish for Honey Nut Cheerios. If your dog's a real cheese nut, cut up some chunks and place them in a party cup with a couple of pennies. Your dog will condition to the rattle of the pennies. Good enough!

must, but no bed until the aggression is gone. In the meantime, until you contact someone (consult your veterinarian), let me give you some food for thought as you strive to resolve your problems.

Advice on Dominant Aggression

Stop being your dog's slave! Ignore all his attempts to get your attention, and do some passive control training to get your dog focused on your direction. Use your Foundation Commands as you lead your dog around on his Teaching Lead, and do not look at him unless he has responded to you. Period. No staring matches unless you've initiated them. Additionally, regulate feedings to twice a day, and do not give food rewards or treats until your problems are gone. Create stations and use them. Go out of your way to get your dog in the way, and then get him out of your way with a big "EXCUSE ME!" This is the most passive way to communicate your leadership. Once a day, do a thirty-minute anchoring session without toys or attention. And call a behaviorist immediately.

❧ *Note: If your dog growls during any of these efforts, such as when you get him to move out of your way, don't push it. Stop everything until you get professional help. Your problem is serious.*

Advice on Spatial Aggression

Proceed with caution. And don't freak out, beat your dog, or scream. These reactions will only reinforce his fearful notion that you've come to compete with his find. In his mind, your dog thinks you've got prize envy. To help your dog accept you as less threatening, follow these steps. I'll use the food dish as an example:

1. Do not make a power struggle out of the feeding ritual. For example, some owners make their dog sit and wait before every meal. This is excessive and encourages food frustration. Ask your dog to sit, and release your dog as you put the bowl down.

2. Shake a box of small dog biscuits, and reward your dog with one. We'll call this the shaker-box. Keep doing this until your dog connects the sound with a reward.

3. Next, approach him once a day with the shaker-box while he is eating a meal. If he growls as you approach him during a meal, stop and toss him a few treats before you leave. Continue doing this until you can stand over him and drop treats into his bowl.

4. At this point, approach his bowl speaking happy praises but without shaking the box. When you get to his side, toss the treat into the bowl and leave.

5. Next, try kneeling down as you shake the box and toss a treat into his bowl.

6. When this passes without tension, try placing the treat into his bowl with your hand.

7. After you've offered your dog a handful of treats, try stirring the kibble with your hand.

8. If you're sucessful, continue procedure this once every other day for a week. Next, after offering a handful of treats, try lifting the bowl. Give it back immediately, and leave. Repeat once a month only.

❖ *Note: If at any point you are frightened or unsure, call a professional. Human fear is suspicious to dogs, and they often act aggressively. I cannot guarantee you will not get bitten in the process. Be your own judge, proceed as long as your dog is comfortable, and call help if necessary.*

PUPPY PREVENTION   To ensure that your puppy gets used to occasional interruptions around her bowl, follow the preceding procedure as a precautionary measure. If your puppy thinks your approach means she's getting something, she'll never be concerned!

PETRA

Petra is a thirteen-month-old Greater Swiss Mountain Dog. She's a happy dog with two loving owners and a brand new seven-week-old human baby brother. Her temperament is delightful, save one big problem. She growls when approached while eating. After questioning her owners, I discovered that Dave, her father, handled the situation by shouting and removing her food dish. But instead of solving the problem, this made it worse. I also learned that Dave had never disciplined Petra for anything else. Poor Petra. Her growling had to do with a natural instinct to protect food. Instead of reassuring her, his reaction created more fear and aggression. Poor Dave, too. He felt horrible as I explained this to him. But after two weeks of following my detailed instructions, he and his wife were able to pass Petra's food dish. Now, instead of growling, she wags her tail and looks for a treat.

Advice on Territorial Aggression

You must assert yourself. Training will be necessary as your dog feels responsible for you. He must be led or stationed during arrivals, and if he is truly out of hand, I suggest you handle him on the chin lead. This collar reduces the negative restraint around the neck and places the body in a submissive posture. When people approach, keep your dog behind you and do not give him any attention until his tension is reduced. You can use the shaker-box to help your dog link up company with a positive reward. Eliminate all yelling or verbose/physical corrections as they add more negative energy to an already-tense situation. To calm your dog, you must set the example.

Advice on Protective Aggression

First, buy a chin lead. Both you and your dog need training. You must learn how to assert dominance over your dog. I remember a client who brought her

Australian Shepard mix into my office. He was so aggressive I couldn't get near either of them. On a hunch, I asked her to toss me the end of the leash and, on the count of three, to run behind the back of the building. Thankfully, I was right. Once the owner was out of sight, the dog's aggression turned into concern about her whereabouts. Fortunately, this owner-dog team worked on a chin lead and followed through with my instructions. They continued training for five weeks. The problem was eventually solved, but not without effort and dedication.

Advice on Predatory Aggression

Most dogs still possess a chasing instinct. Predatory aggression however, usually results in a kill. If you have encouraged your dog's behavior by egging him on, stop. It's not funny. Teach your dog the meaning of "NO," and use it whenever you notice his desire kindling. If you have a Nordic or terrier breed, the only way to correct their killing instinct is to confine them. In other words, you can't. After one of these dogs kills, their desire becomes stronger. This instinct, however, rarely transfers to children. For other solutions, please contact a professional.

Advice on Fear-Induced Aggression

This problem demands a lot of understanding and patience. You cannot correct a fearful dog (you will only increase her fear) or soothe her (your attention will reinforce the behavior). A large part of the problem is that the dog feels no one has control of the situation. To help out, set the example. Keep your dog on her Teaching Lead, and act confident and secure in new situations. Encourage everyone to ignore her until she comes forward. Use your shaker-box to encourage a more positive association to situations.

❧ *Note: Make sure the professional you seek uses a soft and positive approach. Threatening this dog in this situation can create more fear.*

Advice on Dog-to-Dog Aggression

This kind of fighting occurs in two kinds of situations: out-of-home disputes and in-home disputes.

- *Out-of-home disputes* usually are the result of lack of early socialization. The next time around, enroll in a puppy class immediately. In my puppy kindergarten classes, I allow ten minutes of off-lead play. It's a great time for the puppies to socialize with each other and with people. Anyhow, if you've got this problem, you must assess how serious it is. A class might be the perfect solution. You must learn to assert yourself and act as the dominant leader when you meet another dog.

- *In-home disputes* arise when you undermine the hierarchial relationship that develops whenever there are two or more dogs in a home. You will notice the leader. He/she is the one pushing the other dog out of the way when attention is offered, dominating over toys or food, and racing to be out the door first. When you pay more attention to the underdog, the lead dog becomes frustrated and the underdog becomes confused. To calm things down, pay more attention to the Top Dog. Feed, greet, and play with him first and most. Spend time training him. The other dog will follow. If they fight, praise the Top Dog and ignore the other. I know this method sounds cruel, and it *is* hard (I had to do it), but—trust me—it works. If you're having difficulty, bring in a professional.

Aggression is no small problem. And there are no guarantees. If your dog has bitten, you cannot be sure that he won't do it again. Your effort to remedy the problem will only help, however, and this is your only option, save euthanasia. Passing an aggressive dog on to another home or into a shelter would be irresponsible. You'd be responsible if he bit someone else. Get help if you need it. Good luck.

BARKING

Dogs bark for a lot of different reasons. They bark for attention, when they feel threatened, or in defense. Sometimes, dogs bark to communicate play or frustration. Vocal dogs bark at every sound they hear and every motion they see. But to every problem behavior, there is a human element. Understanding your role is the first step in solving your problem.

Attention Barking

This type of barking generally begins at about five months when puppies are in their "bratty" stage. If you paid attention to it then, you're probably paying for it now. I hate to sound like a broken record, but you must ignore your dog to solve this problem. Get up and walk out of the room. Turn the other cheek. Don't cave in. Your dog is trying to train you!

Threatened Barking

If your dog is suddenly startled or frightened by an unsuspecting object or person, she may bark. Don't caress her. Attention reinforces fear. Simply act confident and approach the object or person happily. If you set the example, your dog will follow.

Defensive Barking

You probably want your dog to bark at strangers, but you certainly don't want him to threaten your houseguests. When your dog responds to a knock at the door, don't shout at him or egg him on. Keep him on his Teaching Lead, and say "GOOD DOG, QUIET!" Bring (or station) him behind you as you open the door. Ignore him until he is completely settled down. You're letting your dog know that alarm barking is okay, but the Top Dog (that's you!) ultimately controls the situation.

Play Barking

If your dog starts barking during play, calm her down or refocus her energies on a toy. If you're unsuccessful after ten seconds, end the play session. Next time you play, attach a Short Lead to enforce a calmer attitude.

Frustration Barking

Dogs are not a solitary species. They thrive on group interaction and are frustrated when confined from their group. To communicate this, dogs often resort to barking. And barking often results in attention. Once again, response rewards behavior. The first remedy for this problem is training. Your dog must learn to respond to your barks. Try to keep him with you when you're home, and avoid rescuing a barking dog. Wait until he's settled down. If you

> ## USING SETUPS TO SOLVE PROBLEMS
>
> Ask a friend or family member to stage a doorbell setup. Have them unexpectedly ring the bell while you're practicing with your dog on the Teaching Lead. You'll have complete control. If possible, have them ring the bell at one-minute intervals so that you can condition a proper response in your dog.

have a marathon barker or one you just can't ignore, buy wax ear plugs and get help. No joke!

Sound and Motion Barking

Some dogs are more reactive to unfamiliar sounds and motions than others are. As those of you who have them know, this situation can get out of hand, resulting in a chronic barking problem. To prevent this, teach your dog the meaning of "SPEAK" and "SHHH."

- "SPEAK": Whenever your dog starts barking, use this command and a snappy hand signal (you can make one up) to egg him on.
- "SHHH": After four or five barks, stand tall, and in a low flat voice say "SHHH" as you stamp the floor with your foot. Give the leash a tug, and encourage your dog to follow you by saying his name. Soon you'll be able to get your dog to bark on cue and, more importantly, quiet down on command.

❖ *Note: Don't yell at a barking dog. When you yell, it sounds like you're barking, too! You're having a bark-along, and, in his mind, he started the fun.*

"My Golden Retriver barks during play, but I want her to bark when new people come into the house. What can I do?"

Not much. Golden Retrievers are more concerned with making friends than scaring people off. Teach her to "SPEAK" on cue, and have her bark when she hears someone at the door. Good luck!

"I ignore my dog, but it doesn't work. Whether he's outside or in, he just keeps it up. What about a de-bark collar?"

A diehard. Your dog obviously knows that eventually you'll give in. If you react once in ten times, your dog will bark another ten times. Believe me. I know. I had a barking machine once named Calvin. The first two words he learned were "SPEAK" and "SHHH." I also used a chin lead to handle him. This calmed him tremendously. Next, I bought wax ear plugs. For me. And until he learned better manners, I didn't leave him outside alone. Your dog must learn that you control situations; otherwise he'll think he does and be frustrated when restrained from you. This leads to barking. As for the de-bark collars, I'm not too wild about them. I've permitted two clients to try them pending an eviction. One worked. The other worked for the barking, but made the dog so nervous it starting peeing in the house. Try patience and perseverance instead.

"My puppy whines a lot. What can I do?"

Ignore her. Your puppy is probably entering puberty or adolescence. It is a stressful time, and she's just letting her tensions out. It will pass. If you pay attention to the behavior, however, she'll continue it forever.

CHASING

Chasing is an instinctive behavior that dates back to ancestral times when dogs had to chase prey to survive. Even though we provide their meals and dogs rarely bring down what they chase, it's still a fun pastime and many dogs do it. If you've got a chronic chaser, read closely. You've got some work to do.

Car Chasing

The key in remedying this problem is to think a few steps ahead of your dog. When you sense a car coming, make a big fuss about running to the side of the road. Say "TO THE SIDE" as you run like you're about to be bombed. When you get to the side, instruct your dog to "WAIT" behind you. If he so much as looks at the car, say "NO!" very sternly and snap the leash. You must interrupt the thought process to solve the problem. You should use this same technique with bikes and joggers. Correct your dog the second he thinks about chasing them. Once he's in motion, it's too late.

Cat Chasing

Squirrels, deer and other four-legged animals fall under this heading, too. You'll need a four-legged volunteer, or you can use what the environment provides. Once again, catching the thought process is paramount. The second your dog's ears go up (a sign of anticipation), say "NO" as you snap the lead. Next, place a light twenty-foot line on his buckle collar. When he starts stalking, run in the opposite direction and say "NO" as your dog hits the end of the line.

Child Chasing

This setup requires a few volunteers. Little volunteers, that is. If you haven't got kids, you'll need to borrow some. Here's what you'll do:

1. Place your dog on his Teaching Lead. Keep him standing behind your heels.
2. Ask the children to run in front of you, but watch your dog.
3. As he lowers his head for a lurch, say "NO" sternly and snap back on the lead. *Once again, you correct the thought process!*

When you've mastered this procedure, try some distance control. Place your dog on his Flexi-Leash, and extend your distance from him as your little volunteers race around in front of you. Every time your dog thinks about a chase, correct him by snapping back on the lead, saying "NO," and calling him into a HEEL position.

"I have two dogs who love to chase cars. How can I get them both to stop?"

Buy a coupler. Familiarize yourself with it. It allows you to attach both dogs to the same lead. Next, ask someone to drive while you handle both dogs on the same Teaching Lead. As the person drives by, watch your dogs. As they lower their heads for the chase, say "NO!" and pull them back to your side. Next, run to the curb screaming like you're been hit. Pet them reassuringly when you've made it to the safety zone. Repeat, repeat and repeat until your dogs start running to the curb every time they hear a car. Good dogs!

"My dog no longer chases other people's cars, but when I drive up, she runs at my wheels and jumps at my window."

You're probably paying attention to your dog when she does this. Even negative attention will reinforce this routine. To stop this charade, do the following:

1. Repeat the setup just described, asking your friends to honk the horn when they drive by. Encourage your dog to retreat to the horn sound as well as the car.

2. Have a friend hold your dog on a Flexi-Leash and encourage your dog's retreat as you drive around and honk your horn.

3. Do not yell at your dog. This is interpreted as barking and will spur her on.

4. Have a spray mister of vinegar or Tabasco sauce and water. When your dog jumps on the car, do not look at her. Spritz her face, and stay in the car until she retreats. If you get out when she's jumping, you're reinforcing the jumping. First of all, don't scream at her from the car as you drive up. This will make her wilder.

CHEWING

Like children, dogs are enormously curious about the world around them and they love to explore, especially as puppies. Kids use their hands; dogs use their mouths. Both are capable of going to great lengths to satisfy that curiosity. At around fourteen weeks, puppies begin to teethe. Teething children may keep you up at night, but they will not chew your furniture to alleviate their discomfort. Your puppy might. If your puppy gets attention, even negative, for inappropriate chewing at this stage, his habit may continue into adult doghood. To prevent this nightmare, follow these suggestions:

Provide one chewing object. Given too many toys to choose from, your dog may confuse his objects with yours. Ask your veterinarian's advice as to the best chew toys. I like (for my dogs, not me) pressed rawhide bones or hooves or pig's ears. Pretty unappetizing! Put one in every room and at each station. Offer a bone to your dog if you're talking on the phone, chatting with company or reading the paper.

Keep your dog attached. If you're dealing with a puppy or delinquent chewer, lead or station him on his Teaching Lead to control his rambunctiousness around the house. This enables you to control his actions and keep him out of trouble when he's with you.

Teach your dog to find his bone. In the beginning, command "WHERE'S YOUR BONE?" whenever you give your puppy/dog his bone. Anytime your dog is looking mischievous, clap your hands and ask him "WHERE IS YOUR BONE?" Then help him find it. In a few weeks, you'll notice that he seeks it out on his own.

Once he's got it, it's too late! If your dog already has something in his mouth, you can't correct him. Remember the pencil experiment? Instead, kneel down and enthusiastically encourage your dog to "BRING IT," praising him even if you're less than thrilled with his choice. If he won't come to you, reel him in on his leash or run into the next room. He'll follow you if he thinks there's something more fun around the corner. Remember, dogs don't know good from bad; they just want to have fun and get your attention. If you get angry, he'll learn to hide from you when he finds something. If you encourage him to show you what he's found, he'll bring you all his treasures to share.

Catch the thought process. Read carefully! If you notice your dog showing interest in something he shouldn't (like your shoe, a garbage can or the ever-popular used tissue), startle him by tugging his lead or stamping your foot as you say "NO" in a disciplinary tone. Then pick the object up and correct it. "BAD USED TISSUE! BAD! BAD!" Speak angrily and stare furiously at the object, not your dog. Set up the following situation to discourage interest in a specific item:

1. Place a tempting object on the floor. A crumpled paper towel can be quite irresistible.
2. Bring him to it on his leash.
3. When he approaches, tug back and say "NO!"
4. Pick up the object, shake it forcefully and correct it harshly. "SHAME ON YOU. BAD PAPER TOWEL!" *Look at the object, not the dog.*
5. Toss the object on the ground! Vent your frustrations! Correct it again! It's a very naughty object. Then calmly look to your dog and command, "LET'S GO."

🐾 *Note: If you cannot lift the object, kick it. I know. You'll look ridiculous kicking a roll of toilet paper. But if the method works, hey, use it!*

"My dog baits me. He picks up something he knows is important and stands just out of reach. What can I do?"

Your dog is smart. He has learned what gets your goat. He doesn't really "know" it's important; he just likes to see you in action. First of all, put all treasured objects in a safe place. Next, leave some not-so-important object about, and when your dog takes it, leave. Yes, leave. Walk out of the house, shut the door, and come back in a couple of minutes. Refocus your bewildered dog with a toy, and casually pick up the object. Do not correct your dog for this. Chasing him around communicates only one thing: prize envy. Eventually, this game will lose its magic and cease.

"My dog is no problem until the laundry basket comes out. Then she goes crazy!"

You've got some setting up to do. Here is a thought. Soak a bunch of old socks in Tabasco sauce, fill the basket, and lay a newspaper over the bulk.

Place the sauced socks on top of the paper, and act like it's any other load. (Your dog will get quite a shock this time around. Have a bowl of water awaiting her, but do not soothe her reaction.) Next, spray some Tabasco sauce along the edge of the basket, and correct your dog anytime she thinks about investigating it.

DIGGING

Digging is another favored canine pastime. And like the others, you cannot teach your dog not to dig. Instead, you must give him a place that's all his own. Here are some suggestions:

- Pick one area in which your dog can dig to his heart's content.
- Go to the area ahead of time, and hide some favorite biscuits/toys.
- Go to the area with your dog each day, instructing "GO DIG!"
- Have a dig-feast. Dig with your dog and cheer him on.
- If you catch your dog digging somewhere he shouldn't, correct him with "NO!" and then tell him (escorting him, if necessary) "GO DIG!"

Spraying your dog with a hose or setting mouse traps is cruel, and I don't encourage either. Putting the dirt back into the hole is confusing. Now you're digging in the same spot, too. If you're having a lot of trouble, perhaps you're isolating your dog outside when you're home. This can be very frustrating. Try to structure the environment so that he can be in the house when you're around. Also, when you garden, place your dog indoors. After seeing you dig in one area all day, he may be just too tempted to do the same!

GARBAGE GRABBING

Garbage grabbing gets a lot of attention and is usually very rewarding! To rehabilitate your little garbologist, stop giving him all those after-dinner goodies. I know, I know. It'll go to waste. But if your dog can have it in his bowl, he'll want it in the trash. Next, place your garbage in a confined area if it isn't already. Prevention is the best remedy. If your dog is still rummaging around, try one of the following setups:

- Place your dog on a ten-foot long line, and toss something irresistible into the trash. The second he starts to show interest, step on the line and shout "NO!" Rush up to the can, and kick and scream at it. Do not yell or look at your dog. Go back to whatever you were pretending to do, and repeat the process from the top. If your dog ignores the temptation, give him a hug.
- If your dog is sound-sensitive, construct a pyramid of penny cans. Place ten pennies each in six cans, and arrange them with three on the bottom, two in the middle, and one on top. Tie a string to the middle can on the bottom row, and either attach it to the can or hold it. When your dog shows interest, pull the string and shout "NO!"
- The last thing to try is the balloon stay-away. Blow up a few balloons, and pop them one at a time with a pin with your dog present. As each one pops, act afraid yourself. Don't pay any attention to your dog. Just act it out, and trust me, he'll be watching. Next, tape the balloons to the edge of the garbage can, and leave them there a couple of weeks.

"My dog is an angel when we're in the room. It's when we leave that he gets into trouble."

A wise guy. Mr. Clever. There are several approaches you can try:

1. Set up a bitter-tasting lure by soaking a paper towel in Tabasco sauce. Repeat this until he loses interest in the trash.
2. Set up the penny-can pyramid, and booby trap him when you've left the room.
3. Set up a deflective mirror so that you can keep your eye on the garbage can even when you're not physically present. When you see your dog approaching, storm in and correct his thought process.

HOUSEBREAKING

Whether you're starting with a puppy or an older dog, following every detail of this housebreaking plan is essential for success. In general, dogs are clean creatures who prefer absorbent surfaces and don't like to hang out where they eliminate. Their clean nature makes the housebreaking process easier.

Here are the guidelines.

Confinement

The fastest way to house-train your puppy is to keep an eye on her. Either use the Training Lead or crate/isolate her (a less desirable alternative). You may allow short bouts of freedom if she has emptied herself and you have the time to pay close attention to her.

Young Pups

Puppies under twelve weeks of age cannot separate their thought to go to the bathroom from the action of doing so. Don't correct a young dog. They'll catch on as they grow up. Young dogs need to go out after a meal, a nap, play, or isolation. Watch them closely during these times.

Food

Ask your veterinarian to help you select a good kibble and a feeding schedule. When feeding time arrives, place the food and water bowls down for fifteen minutes, then remove them. If your dog can't stay still for the allotted time, crate or station her with her bowls. If she doesn't eat, don't worry! She may need to skip a meal or two before she gets in the habit of eating at mealtimes. It is easier to housebreak a dog on a consistent feeding schedule. Her last feeding should be somewhere between 4:00 P.M. and 6:00 P.M. as it takes about six hours for her bowels to cycle.

Water

Make water available during feedings. Additionally, have water available before you take your dog to the bathroom. Don't give her free access to water yet, or your dog may turn into a fountain. Remove all water after 7:30 P.M. If you think she's thirsty, give her some ice cubes, as they absorb faster into the bloodstream.

Creating a Routine

Get your dog focused on a routine, and encourage everyone helping out to follow the rules. Here are the elements involved in your routine:

Pick "The Door": Pick one door through which to take your dog outside. Each time you go to the door, command "OUTSIDE." Repeat it every three second until you are at The Spot.

Pick "The Spot": Designate a five-foot-by-five-foot area in your yard or house as The Spot. If you're outside-training, locate the area near the door. If you're paper-training, cover a large area, slowly decreasing its size until it's appropriate for your puppy's needs.

Pick "The Command": Use a short, snappy command like "GET BUSY" or "DO IT" when your dog squats to eliminate. Say it once or twice, and praise her calmly when she finishes. You'll appreciate this command when she wants to go out in the pouring rain at 4:00 o'clock in the morning.

No Free Rides

Avoid carrying your dog to her spot. This is something she must learn to do herself!

First Things First

When you wake up in the morning or come home at night, don't greet your dog until after she has eliminated. Put her lead on, and walk her to her spot, commanding "OUTSIDE!" As she goes, command "GET BUSY," then greet her happily and either play or go for a walk.

The Outside Routine

Your dog will need to go out after feeding, exercising, napping and isolation. Use the following chart as a guide:

Age	Trips to the Spot
6 to 14 weeks	8 to 10
14 to 20 weeks	6 to 8
20 to 30 weeks	4 to 6
30 weeks to adulthood	3 to 4

Corrections

Do not hit or yell at your dog if she makes a mistake. A lot of people want to know how to correct a dog after the fact. "Does the old discipline of rubbing their noses in it still work?" No, it doesn't. I can think of nothing more disgusting. If you didn't catch her in time, you're the one who must take responsibility. Remove her from the room, and clean the area with a 50-50 mix of white vinegar and water. Do not clean the area in front of her. The only time you can correct your dog is if you catch her in the thought process or just as she's starting to go. Then startle her by making an unfamiliar, guttural "EH, EH, EH!" sound, and command "OUTSIDE!" You want your dog to think the ceiling is falling when she eliminates indoors but that everyone is so happy when she goes to her place. Be patient. She'll get there.

Deciphering Her Signal

Before you take this step, make sure your dog understands the routine. One morning, take her to the door on-lead without commanding "OUTSIDE." Don't say anything—no pats or eye contact—just walk her to the door. Stand still and pay attention. She's accustomed to marching right out, so she may start whining, jumping or pulling. When she does, call her back to you and say "OUTSIDE!" When her body language says "YES! YES! OUTSIDE!" praise her and take her to her spot. When she catches on that she must give you a sign before you go outside, start using this system in rooms farther away from the door.

"My dog doesn't give any signal. She just sits and watches me until I take her out."

You'll have to watch for subtle signs and then praise her wildly before going out. This will encourage a more revved-up reaction. If she shows absolutely no sign, jump around a little (encouraging a bark or a jump) before you say "OUTSIDE." Soon she'll pick up the routine.

"Where should I put the crate?"

Ideally, in a bedroom. If you're concerned about messes, lay paper underneath. Being around you makes your dog calmer and more receptive to sleeping through the night.

"My dog eliminates in the crate. What should I do?"

(Check with your veterinarian to make sure your dog doesn't have a urinary tract infection or worms.) Perhaps your crate is too big. If so, make it smaller. You can buy crate dividers, or you can rig one yourself. Additionally, remove all absorbent material from the crate. Some dogs love to pee on absorbent things. If you're still having problems, find a professional behaviorist/trainer; your dog may be suffering from Separation Anxiety.

"My ten-week-old Cairn Terrier wakes up at 3 A.M. and whines. Should I take him out?"

Yes, but don't make a big thing of it. Take him to his spot, bring him back in, and go back to bed. Period. Though his bladder is too small to make it through the night, if you play games at 3 A.M., he'll keep getting up at 3 A.M.

"Will I have to crate my dog forever?"

Not unless you want to. Eventually, when your dog can hold his urine, try stationing (see Chapter 3). Once sleeping at his station has become a habit, leashing him will not be necessary.

"My dog just wants to play outside. He thinks the carpet is for peeing."

Do not walk around or play with your dog when you take him out. Calmly walk to the selected area, stand still, and ignore your dog until he has gone to the bathroom. If he doesn't do anything for five minutes, take him back inside, ignore him, and crate or lead him for fifteen to thirty minutes. Once your dog eliminates outside, praise him and play a favorite game. Soon he'll learn that going outside begins playtime!

INEDIBLE INGESTION (PICA)

"My dog is constantly scrounging around outside and eats everything, even plastic bags and bottlecaps. Is it safe?"

No, it's not safe. It's called inedible ingestion (professionally known as pica). If the problem persists, bring it to the attention of your veterinarian, and/or call in a professional. To resolve this problem, you must work hard at controlling your behavior. Yes, your behavior. If you scream and chase your dog every time he reaches for something, you're actually encouraging him to continue. It's that prize envy concept again. You look like a mad dog threatening your dog for a treasure. Only two alternatives for your dog: run fast or gulp the evidence.

Remember, get help if you need it, but until then try these measures:
- Keep your dog leashed outside until the problem subsides.
- Teach your dog to "WAIT" at all doorways, the first step in self control.
- Once your dog has learned "HEEL," use it as you walk and discourage all sniffing.
- Bring along a distraction toy like the fishing rod described in Chapter 2 ("Fishing with Fido") and play with it when you walk.
- Each time you dog sniffs at garbage, spritz the object indiscreetly with Bitter Apple or another disgusting liquid and say "NO" calmly but firmly. Continue walking in an upbeat manner.

🐾 *Note: Do not get tense or angry at your dog if he beats you to something and swallows it. Call you veterinarian and watch his digestion carefully. Do not pick up anything in front of him, because if you "eat it," he'll want to do the same.*

JUMPING

Everybody knows a jumper. Little jumpers and big jumpers. Wild, knock-over-the-furniture jumpers and the muddy-paw-print-on-your-pants jumpers.

The most popular excuse for this behavior is "He's just saying hello!" Not true! He's saying "Thank you for teaching me this excellent way of getting attention! I'll do this again and again and again!"

Let's take a closer look. All dogs start out as attention-seeking puppies. And it's true, all puppies are irresistible. When they jump, they get lots of love, plenty of attention and a few kisses to boot!

Puppy Lesson #1: Jumping is an interactive behavior, definitely worth repeating! But as puppies gets bigger, their charm wears off. They get pushed and shouted at for a behavior that was once encouraged.

Puppy Lesson #2: Jumping is still interactive, still worth repeating! She continues to jump; you continue to push. Jump, push. Jump, push. Help!

To rehabilitate your jumper, follow these suggestions:

1. Never look at or touch a jumping dog. Any attention, even a glance, reinforces the behavior.
2. Practice "SIT." A lot! Position your dog if she does not respond. Don't repeat yourself.
3. Keep your dog on the Teaching Lead or the Short Lead at all times.

Dogs jump for a whole variety of reasons. Each situation requires a different response.

Attention Jumpers

If your dog jumps on you for attention, ignore her. It can be as simple as that. If she's unbearable, grab her lead or collar and snap down firmly while you continue to ignore her. When she gets down, pause for at least five seconds, instruct "SIT" and pet her. Soon she'll catch on that sitting is the new rage.

Greeting Jumpers

When you greet your dog after an absence, stay calm! Mom's right again: Good manners start at home. If you go nuts, you're teaching your dog to be hog-wild when the door opens. Instead, give her a special bone and ignore her until she settles down. If she's banging around in her crate, don't open it until she's quiet. Instruct "SIT" when she gets a grip, and pet her gently. Reinforce calmness, and you'll be doing both of you, not to mention your guests, a favor!

Company Jumpers

When company arrives, either lead her to greet them or station her six to ten feet from the door. Tell her "WAIT" as you open the door and give her a special toy (one she gets only when company comes in). You'll need to train your company, too. Insist that they ignore your dog until she's calm. Even if she barks or attempts to jump. If she does leap forward, snap her down in midair as you say "NO!" Repeat this as often as necessary, and continue to ignore her. When she settles down, bring her and her toy over to your company. Hold her in a sit position while they pet her. As you visit with your guests, anchor your dog at your side and give her a special toy.

Furniture Fanatics

You must decide right now if you want a furniture dog. Do you want your full-grown dog jumping on the couch, sitting in your favorite chair, hogging the bed? If that sounds like your plan, read no further. But if you'd rather have your dog on the floor, read on. Create a place on the floor near your furniture. Encourage her to "SETTLE DOWN" by placing a comfortable bed and a favorite chew. Praise your dog when she lies quietly or chews. If your dog continues to jump, station her or attach a short lead and snap her off each time, saying "NO!" Tell her to "SETTLE DOWN" in her place, praising her when she does.

A tip for puppy owners: Control yourselves! Puppies are so irresistible. I know it's hard to keep them on the floor, but you must start now. You can still cuddle to your heart's content; just get down on the floor to do it!

Counter Culprits

Not all dogs choose human targets. Some find the defrosting turkey on your kitchen counter to be far more interesting and will perform mind-boggling gymnastic feats to get it. If you have a counter culprit, set up a tempting situation. Put your dog on her Teaching Lead, and get some tasty human food from the fridge. If she even pauses to consider what's on the counter, tell her

"NO!" firmly and snap back on the lead. Quickly turn back to the subject of interest and correct it, not your dog, firmly. "BAD TURKEY! BAD! BAD!"

"Can't I ever let my dog jump on me?"

Believe it or not, yes. But not now. First you must teach her not to jump. Once she understands that, you can instruct "UP!" and let her jump with your permission. If she tries it without permission, ignore her as you snap her away.

"What do I do when my dog jumps at me when he's on leash?"

Are you holding the collar too tightly? That can be frightening for dogs who feel like they're being hung. If that checks out, your dog is probably confronting your control. Don't buy it. Try ignoring him completely. Try it, wearing an old coat if you have to. If your dog still persists, carry a spray mister of vinegar/water and spray your dog indiscreetly while you continue walking. Don't face your dog, as this posture reinforces his confrontational efforts.

"Some corrections make my dog wilder. What am I doing wrong?"

It sounds like your dog isn't taking you too seriously. You'll need to do some foundation training to get him focused on you. Are you bending over to correct him, yelling, or using your hands to push him away? All these corrections are interactive and encourage rougher play. Perhaps your dog just has a lot of energy or needs to go to the bathroom. Check it out.

"My dog ignores the counter when we're around, but as soon as we turn our back, she jumps right up. It seems like a game."

An opportunist! Try stationing your dog for a while, telling him to "WAIT" as you leave the room. Then try the same setup without stationing. Also correct the surfaces your dog shows interest in.

"I have a Toy Poodle, and I don't mind her jumping."

You may not mind, but your houseguests might. Teach your dog to ask permission to come up. When she jumps, ignore her temporarily, and then when she gets down, instruct "SIT." Next, instruct "UP!" and lift her into your lap. Soon she'll come and sit for permission instead of jumping. Remember, a well-mannered dog can be selectively spoiled!

MOUNTING

Don't be too embarrassed. Mounting is more a sign of dominance than of sexual preference. This, however, makes it no more acceptable. Mounting dogs are bossy dogs who get overstimulated in exciting situations. To rehabilitate yours, do the following:

1. Leave a short lead on your dog.
2. Do not face off to a mounting dog. No eye contact or pushing.
3. When the mounting starts, calmly grasp the short lead and snap down firmly.
4. Once your dog is grounded, stand very tall, glare at your dog, and say "SHAME ON YOU" in your most indignant tone. Station your dog for fifteen minutes with no attention.
5. If your dog is mounting other dogs or the kids, keep your approach calm and repeat the preceding procedure. Do not storm into the situation.

🐾 *Note: If your dog acts aggressively, terminate the corrections and seek help.*

"Why does my eleven-month-old male Husky mount my eight-year-old Labrador-mix. What's going on?"

It's a dominance issue. Nothing more. Let them work it out. And once they've established dominance, support it. See "Multi-dog Households" in the Appendix.

NIPPING/MOUTHING

Puppy nipping is natural. Until fourteen weeks. After this time, nipping symbolizes control play and isn't permissible; it's pushy. To stop this behavior, follow these guidelines:

- Eliminate all tug-of-war and wrestling games. Period. They encourage nipping and aggressive play.
- Any time your puppy/dog licks you, command "KISSES" and praise him.
- Young puppies (under fourteen weeks) are naturally oral. They nipped their mother softly when they were weaned. She tolerated soft mouthing without recognition, but if they nipped too hard, she gave them a clear message to back off. When puppy siblings played, they nipped each other, too. Rough play and hard nipping elevated a puppy's position in the group hierarchy. When you bring your puppy home, he wants to know whether you're the mother figure or a littermate. To communicate leadership, ignore all soft mouthing. Yes, ignore it. If you screech or pull your hand away, you're reinforcing it with attention and submissive puppy play. If your puppy bites down hard, say "NO!" forcefully and pull your puppy's head from your hand. I repeat: *Pull your puppy's head from your hand.* Command "KISSES," praising your puppy if he does. If your puppy is getting wild, refocus his energy with a toy. See the Puppy section of the appendix for other suggestions.

🐾 *Note: At this age, puppies like to interact around your face. Yes, it is a sign of affection, but they also bite faces in play. Don't let your puppy near your face when he's excited. Puppy play bites can hurt!*

- As your puppy matures (when he's older than fourteen weeks), you must teach him not to place his mouth on human skin. There are two corrections you can try: 1) Place your puppy/dog on a short lead, and correct any and all mouthing by snapping his head away firmly with the lead or collar and saying "NO." Remember, don't pull your hand out of his mouth as it will encourage rougher play. Act indignant, and yank that mouth away! 2) Buy and fill travel mister pumps (from the pharmacy) with a vinegar/water mixture (if this is ineffective, try lemon juice or Tabasco sauce or mouth spray). Keep plenty around the house and some in your pocket. Whenever your dog mouths, say "NO" while you indiscreetly spray him on the muzzle. Do not move your hand from his mouth. Encourage "KISSES" and then praise your dog. If he ignores you, ignore him.

"I've tried various corrections, like holding my five-month-old puppy's mouth shut or smacking his snout. They seem to make the situation worse."

Your puppy perceives these corrections as confrontational play. I don't encourage these methods. I find that acting indignant and shameful works better. Pull your puppy's mouth away from your hand. If he just won't quit, walk away.

"I have three kids and one dog. They love to wrestle, but they don't like it when Buddy (my seven-month-old Keeshond) plays too rough. Help!!!"

They're small. They're energetic. They love to race around and play games. And I'm not talking about your dog! It's easy for dogs raised with children to mistake these little creatures for other puppies, and that can lead to some pretty wild behavior—on both their parts. You're faced with a double whammy: training your dog and controlling the kids.

- Anytime your kids can't slow down, you should station, crate or lead your dog away from them.
- Avoid getting angry or frustrated at either of them. Your energy will only excite or frighten your dog. Help your kids see that overenthusiasm ends play time.
- Put your dog on his Teaching Lead, and encourage the kids to run in front of you. If your dog starts to charge, snap the lead and say "NO!" Repeat this until your dog watches them calmly.

- Small children may pull on your dog's coat or explore around his face. Condition your dog to accept this handling by praising him while you gently pull his coat and handle his face. He'll be more accepting of the children if you accustom him to such treatment first.
- Encourage your kids to play with your dog when he's calm or chewing a bone. Make this a special time with you and your kids. Reward both for being calm!

SEPARATION ANXIETY

Separation aniexty can result in destructive chewing, house soiling or excessive barking. It's an all-too-common problem. There are two situations that encourage it: passivity and dominance.

The Passive Dog: This dog clings to his owners when they are home, often soliciting attention and getting it. This leads to over-identification, not too unlike a child who clings to his mother's leg. This dog is confused about himself and depends on your presence to reassure him. When you're gone, the anxiety sets in.

The Dominant Dog: This fellow thinks he is king of his castle. Ruler of the roost. When his owners, whom he considers his subordinates, leave, his anxiety is in their best interest. "How will they survive without their great leader there to protect them?"

To resolve this problem, in either case, the dog must be trained. For the passive dog, training will help him feel he has a secure leader and a personality all his own; for the dominant dog, training will place him in a subordinate, carefree pack-position. If you need help training, get it. In the meantime, follow these ground rules:

Never correct your dog after the fact. Never. Your dog will associate corrections not with the destruction but with your arrival. Therefore, he will be more anxious the next time you leave.

Avoid theatrical hellos and goodbyes. Lavishing your dog with kisses, biscuits and drawn-out declarations of devotion do not reassure him. They stress him out.

Leave a radio playing classical music to cover unfamiliar sounds.

Place your dog in a dimly lit area to encourage sleep.

Leave a favorite chew toy with him. Rub it between your palms for scent.

If you're leaving for over six hours, try to find someone to walk your dog. Otherwise, proof the house against his destruction by purchasing an indoor pen. They fold nicely so that you can store them away when you're home, and they can be expanded before you leave to give your dog space when you are gone for extended periods. Dogs get cramped when left in small kennels for over six hours and develop hyper isolation anxiety.

When home, temporarily decrease your physical attention by 50 percent. Do not give in to solicitations. Although it relieves your guilty feelings, it is too sharp a contrast from being left alone all day. When alone, your dog longs for the companionship, and since chewing fingernails or watching the soaps isn't an option, he may settle for your couch.

If possible, buy a kitten for your dog. Kittens are super companions, and they are great company for dogs if raised with them. Getting another dog is also an option, though it's better to wait until you've resolved this problem.

The next step in remedying his anxiety is a series of practice departures. Station your dog in a familiar spot. Instruct "WAIT." Leave the room for fifteen seconds. Return. Ignore him until he's settled, then praise him lovingly. Repeat this procedure ten times or until he's stays calm. Continue these short separations until he shows no anxiety. Double the separation time, and repeat the procedure. Continue doubling the departure time until you're able to leave the room for thirty minutes.

Once he's comfortable for thirty minutes, go back to short separations, but, this time, leave the house. Gradually work your way up to spending thirty minutes out of the house. Then start over; this time, get into and start your car. With patience, you'll be able to build his confidence and leave him for longer and longer periods of time.

If you seek help, make sure you avoid trainers who encourage discipline.

"Why is training so important?"

Think of your dog as a kid. Kids need parents. If they don't have them, they lose their sense of themselves and behave in a frightened or manic fashion. Dogs need a leader, like kids need a parent. Training communicates that you're applying for the position. Successful training takes a lot of pressure off your dog. Someone else is on the lookout. Someone else is in control. Your dog thinks: *I can just relax. I can just be a dog. I don't have to be the leader.*

STIMULATED SPRINKLING

Sprinkling comes in two forms: submissive or excitement. If your puppy is doing this, don't worry. It's normal. If you've got an older dog, your problem may be more serious, though it is usually resolvable. First of all, never correct your dog. She has no idea she's doing it. Corrections make it worse. To solve your problem, follow the appropriate measures:

1. When you come in, ignore your dog until she's completely calm.
2. Command "SIT" before petting.
3. Kneel down to pet her, rather than leaning over.

If your dog is timid with certain people, have everyone (including yourself) ignore her. If you soothe her, you reinforce her fear. When your dog approaches the person, offer her treats (you can use a shaker-box). If she is calm, have the person kneel and pet her chest.

If your dog piddles during greetings or play sessions, ignore her or stop the play until she has better bladder control.

> *"I have a four-month-old puppy who is very shy and three young kids. The kids are rough and frighten the pup. When he's frightened, he pees. And it's getting worse. Is it possible that the puppy is unsuited for our chaotic household?"*

Yes, it is. I can't tell based on your written statement, but you may want to get an unbiased and professional opinion. If so, the fairest alternative for both you and the pup is to find him a home in a more passive household. Perhaps with an older couple. If you decide to get another puppy, do more research into temperament and breed type. Test your new candidate before you bring him home. Pick one with a strong sense of self. Good luck.

STOOL SWALLOWING (COPROPHAGIA)

Dogs swallow two kinds of stools: other creatures' stools and their own stools. Both behaviors are pretty disgusting. But, believe it or not, neither is that unnatural.

OTHER CREATURES' STOOLS   These are actually quite a delicacy. For dogs. They find them tasty. Corrections, unfortunately, make it worse. Your dog will think you want it, too. So he gulps faster. Most dogs outgrow this behavior if you feed them a balanced meal twice a day and ignore their stool fetish. Try to refocus your dog on a favorite activity. If you're suffering from litter box blues, put the litter box in an inaccessible area or correct the box as outlined in the "Chewing" section of this chapter. There's only one thing to be happy about in this situation. Be happy you're not a dog!

THE DOG'S OWN STOOLS   Though this is probably the most grotesque thing you could ever think about, in dogland it's just a handy way to keep the den clean. When your dog was a puppy, he watched his mother do it, and when he sees you cleaning up after him, he thinks . . . well, you get the picture. To halt this habit, try the following:

1. Don't correct your dog when he shows interest in his stool. If you fuss, he'll gulp.
2. If your dog's showing interest, refocus him on a favorite game. "Get your ball!"
3. Ask your veterinarian to give you a food additive that will make the dog's feces distasteful to him. I know, what's more distasteful than dog poop? But such things do exist.
4. After your dog is finished eliminating, spray the pile with something distasteful such as Bitter Apple, Tabasco sauce or vinegar.

TIMIDITY

Timid dogs look so pitiful. You just want to soothe them, like you soothe kids. But dogs are not kids, and they'll think your soothing is a sign of your fear. Now you're both afraid. That's a big problem.

To help your dog, you must act confident when she is afraid. You're the leader. Stand up straight. Relax your shoulders. Smile. Whether it's a bag blowing in the wind, a sharp noise (like thunder), or an uncommon face, act calm, face the feared object, and ignore your dog until she starts to act more like you.

🐾 *Note: If your dog is showing aggression when she's fearful, call for help. Do not knowingly put her in "threatening situations."*

"Speaking of thunder, what do I do when it strikes? My dog is a nervous wreck."

Let me start with the don'ts. Don't coddle your dog. Don't permit him to hide between the sheets or climb onto the couch. Don't isolate him. These make the fear worse. Depending on how bad your situation is, try one or all of these approaches:

- Turn on some classical music, and play it loudly.
- Lead your dog on his Teaching Lead while you act completely calm. Set the example. Show him how to cope with the situation. Let your dog have his fears, just don't respond to them. When he calms down, pet him lovingly.
- Find (or make) a thunderstorm tape recording. Play it on low volume while you play your dog's favorite game with him. Slowly increase the volume.
- Ask your veterinarian for tranquilizers to soothe him before a storm.

APPENDIX

1. PUPPIES

Whoever started the rumor that puppies are so cute they make perfect gifts and spur-of-the-moment purchases, please sit down. Puppies are a lot of work and a tremendous responsibility! But they can be a lot of fun, too! Here are some hints to help you along:

PUPPIES AND BABIES Babies are a great point of reference in raising a pup—or vice versa. Both are a lot alike. They go through developmental stages, need to be pottied, and have to be taught good manners. When they are young, they are focused more on themselves and their own needs than on you. And, last but not at all least, they learn best by positive reinforcement and structure rather than harsh discipline. The main difference between them and us is that puppies use their mouths instead of their hands to explore their world. Remember this as he's mouthing everything in sight. It's natural. Completely natural.

PUPPIES UNDER TWELVE WEEKS A puppy less than twelve weeks old is like a child less than a year old. Corrections don't make sense. Would you yell at a ten-month-old for grabbing your earring or swiping the crystal off the dining room table? I hope not. Your efforts would be as fruitless with a young pup. They're going to nip and chew just like a baby pulls and grabs. All you can do for now is patiently remove whatever you don't want them to touch and redirect their attention.

IT'S A PUPPY   I know. Puppies can be really frustrating. They chew, jump, nip, and pee where they're not supposed to, but after all they're just puppies and that's what puppies do. They're not acting out of spite or to make you angry, so try to calm down. Harsh corrections or yelling will only frighten your puppy or, worse, egg him on.

SNOWFLAKES   Like snowflakes, puppies are unique. Your puppy will have his own special personality, which will determine how you communicate with him. Does he have a passive or active temperament?

Passive puppies like direction and shrink from making independent decisions. They feel most secure and calm near their group. If you've got a passive puppy, train him with a gentle hand and avoid corrections. Ignore all anxious, shy or fearful responses, as your attention will reinforce them. Passive puppies can develop into sweet, gentle, adoring pets if they're handled properly. If given too much attention for shy or insecure behavior, however, they may develop Separation Anxiety or chronic timidity.

Active puppies have a strong sense of themselves. They are outgoing, unafraid and funny. Training and moderate corrections may be needed to focus their attention. Always a part of things, they can make a dynamic addition to any household. Left untrained or isolated, they can be very disruptive, annoying and destructive.

NEEDS   Puppies under nine months are motivated by five primary needs, which are the following:
1. Hunger
2. Thirst
3. Sleep
4. Energy
5. Elimination

If at any point they have a need that is not been met, you'll know about it. They will act out. Some dogs will bark or whine; others will nip or jump. If your dog is acting up and just won't quit, ask yourself: "Could he be trying to tell me something?"

MATURITY   Like babies and tadpoles, your puppy will grow up. Before you know it, he'll stop chasing every blowing leaf and will grow accustomed to the long wagging thing at the end of his body. If you handled his youth correctly, his maturity will bring a consistency to your world that will go unchecked by seasons or time. He will truly be a Best Friend.

2. KIDS AND DOGS

I once gave a lecture titled "Kids and Dogs: Constant Companion or Sibling Rivals?" in which I stressed that raising children and dogs together may not be as effortless as those reruns of Lassie and Timmy might lead one to believe. Both creatures are in need of constant attention and care, and it is crucial that a child be encouraged to help with the family pet. (Don't get me wrong. I think dogs can make wonderful companions for children, but there are hidden responsibilities and considerations to keep in mind.) 🐾 *Tip: Encouraging children to help care for the family dog helps reinforce a constant companion relationship, whereas punishing them for rough play could create a rivalry.*

HELP!   Know when to ask for it. If your dog is becoming less tolerant of your child, showing signs of aggression, or creating such havoc that your normal daily tasks and parental responsibilities are stressed, call a trainer or behaviorist immediately. They can really help. Ask your veterinarian for a referral.

ATTENTION-ATTENTION!   Kids love it as much as dogs do, and like dogs they're not concerned whether it's negative or positive. A lot of times children will tease their dog just to get their parent's attention. Keeping this in mind with your family, praise all positive interactions. Take time to notice

EXPECTING A BABY?

Congratulations! Here are some tips to get your four-footed family member ready for the new arrival.

Carry a doll around the house. If you can find one that cries or eats, go for the big effect! Use a SIT-STAY as you pretend to change the diaper and a SETTLE DOWN when you feed.

Keep your dog with you as you prepare the baby's room. Create a station area for him in the corner or right outside the door so that you won't have to exclude him when the baby comes. Exclusion can cause new-infant-resentment syndrome, and you wouldn't want that!

You've given birth! A miracle to behold. Before you come home, ask a spouse, friend or family member to show your dog a used bed cloth or diaper. Familiarizing him with the scent will help him feel more comfortable when the baby arrives.

Your homecoming. The big day. To help your dog ease into the transition, ask someone to handle him on his lead as you come through the door. If you feel up to it, let someone hold the child and greet him as usual. After he's calmed down, allow him to sniff nearby as you praise and treat him lovingly. The start of a beautiful relationship!

your child when he pets the dog calmly or helps out with the feedings. If you see any rough play or teasing, calmly remove your dog from the situation and isolate him in a crate or private room. Don't discipline the dog; just remove him peacefully. Ignore your child for fifteen minutes to let him know that rough play ends interaction time.

TEASING   Children, especially those under eight years of age, tease dogs. It's a fact of life. Though teasing can be minimized, it can't be eliminated entirely. To help your dog get accustomed to the way children treat animals, mimic it yourself. Pry your dog's mouth open, handle her feet, tug her coat, and, as you do, praise her and give her treats. The next time you catch your child handling her, praise them both, and let your child be the one to give her a treat! ❧ *Tip: You can teach children not to tease through the power of your example and positive reinforcement of calm interactions.*

DOG STRESS?   Is your young child or baby stressing your dog out? Does he jump when your child crawls across the floor? Does he dodge oncoming toddlers? If so, he needs help overcoming his anxieties. Try praising and treating him every time the child is near. Acting happy will give him a good feeling and dislodge all those old tensions. I know, it may be nerve-wracking, but a negative response communicates anxiety and puts a real strain on their relationship. Act happy and he'll be happy!

CARING FOR THE FAMILY DOG   Although children under five cannot be expected to perform any care duties without help, older children and other household members can and should assume some of the responsibilities. To encourage everyone's participation, make a fun project out of all the necessary duties (brushing, feeding, walking and exercise) and design a special roster to hang on your refrigerator (see my sample). Be creative in your encouragement, and avoid getting angry for lack of cooperation. Anger is, after all, just another form of attention. We're not so unlike our dogs after all!

❧ *Note: You are your children's best example. If you're calm and structured with your dog or puppy, your child will copy you. If you're frantically confused or you encourage rough play, your child will copy that behavior, too. The choice is up to you.*

3. MULTI-DOG HOUSEHOLDS

Having two dogs can be twice the fun! Or it can be double the trouble. The decision is in your hands. Here are some hints for making it easier:

A DOG IS A DOG IS A DOG   Truer words were never spoken. Certain similarities string them all together. Like us, however, each has a unique personality and temperament that will affect the way they relate to their world. In a multi-dog household, everyone must be sensitive to the needs of each individual dog.

HIERARCHY Personality also affects the way dogs relate to one another. In a group of two or more dogs, a hierarchy will develop, with the most outgoing, assertive dog assuming the Top-Dog rank.

WHO'S YOUR TOP DOG?

To determine who is your Top Dog, observe your group's behavior. The Top Dog is the one who insists on being the first through the door, barges the others out of the way for attention, and ends up with all the toys in her lap. There is no sexism in dogland. You may be surprised that your female is running the show!

ROYALTIES Once your dogs develop a hierarchy, you must support it by giving all the household royalties to your Top Dog. She should be fed, greeted, petted and allowed out first. If you pay more attention to the subordinate dog, you may cause discontent among the ranks, which may lead to fighting.

SAME AGE Raising two dogs of the same age can be quite a challenge. Resolving housebreaking, chewing, nipping, or jumping habits can double your work load. You'll have to pay close attention and be very consistent.

On the other hand, raising two dogs can also be twice the fun if you're considerate of their individual needs and train them to be more focused on you than on each other. Often, when raised together, puppies will develop opposing personalities. The more outgoing one assumes Top-Dog rank, while the other dog is more passive. Although it's tempting to console the introvert, remember the Laws of Nature, which instruct you to defer all royalties to the Top Dog, and the Attention Factor, which reminds you that if you pay attention to an introverted dog, you'll get an introverted dog. Here are some other hints to prevent future problems:

1. Left alone twenty-four hours a day, your puppies will form a strong bond to each other and be less attached to you. To prevent this, separate them at least twice a day. If possible, let them sleep in separate bedrooms.

2. Use individual crates for housebreaking, chewing or sleeping difficulties.

3. Feed the puppies separately. If you feed them together, the Top Dog puppy may horde the food.

4. Support their hierarchy. Feed, pet and greet the stronger dog first.

DIFFERENT AGES   "Monkey see, monkey do" could not apply more. Puppies raised with older dogs pick up a lot of their habits. Both good and bad. To discourage the younger dog from bad behavior, resolve your older dog's problems first. In addition, follow the same suggestions described in the preceding section.

If you've welcomed a mature dog into your pack, you'll need to observe the new hierarchy and respect it. When I brought my Labrador into my family, he quickly dominated my eight-year-old Husky. Though this arrangement broke my heart initially, once I supported their system, everybody was happy.

DISCIPLINE   If you don't know who did it, you can't correct either. That's the rule. If you find a mess after the fact, forget it. Disciplining your dogs will only weaken your connection to them and strengthen their resolve to one another. For suggestions on specific problems, see Chapter 7.

IS WRESTLING OK?   Yes, to a degree. Try to teach your dogs to go to certain areas of the house or outside to play. If they're out of hand, leave their Short Leads on in the house and correct them by saying "SSHHH!" as you pull them apart sternly. Instruct "SIT," and refocus them on a chew toy.

THE NAME GAME   Teach your dogs two names: their personal name, and a universal one that you can use when they're together. "DOGS!" "GIRLS!"

"BOYS!" "BABIES!" Whatever works for you. This system simplifies things when you have to call them. "BUDDY, COME!" rolls off a little easier than "BUDDY, FI-FI, DAISY, MARLO, COME!"

FEEDINGS   Feed your dogs separately. Place your Top Dog's bowl down first. If you're having difficulty keeping them separate, station them apart on their Teaching Leads.

TOY WAR   I know. You want them both to have a toy, but one dog keeps insisting on having both. You give the toy back to the other dog, and the Top Dog takes it away. Give-take-give-take. Remember your Top-Dog rule. If the Top Dog wants both, he gets both. Period.

DOG FIGHTS   Whatever you do, don't yell! Yelling is perceived as threat barking and will actually make the problem worse. If you have a dog fight, the best thing to do is walk out of the house and slam the door. No words or discipline, just an abrupt departure. It's usually your presence that prompts an argument. You can also try breaking up the fight by dumping a bucket of water on their heads or turning a hose on them. Once things are calmed down, review your actions. Were you supporting the underdog? That's not good. After the fight has been settled, you should isolate the subordinate and praise the Top Dog. I know it sounds cruel, but if Number One feels supported, he won't challenge the other dogs. Additionally, if you catch a fight before it begins, shame the underdog and reward your Top Dog with attention. I know it feels unnatural, but remember that your dogs aren't human and they don't think you are, either. If the situation reoccurs, call in a professional.